IMAGINARY
CHRISTS

IMAGINARY CHRISTS

The Challenge of Christological Pluralism

RICHARD GRIGG

State University
of New York
Press

Published by
State University of New York Press, Albany

Production by Susan Geraghty
Marketing by Anne M. Valentine

Printed in the United States of America

For information, address State University of New York
Press, State University Plaza, Albany, N.Y., 12246

Library of Congress Cataloging-in-Publication Data

Grigg, Richard, 1955–
    Imaginary Christs : the challenge of christological pluralism / Richard Grigg.
       p.   cm.
    Includes bibliographical references and index.
    ISBN 0-7914-4647-6 (hardcover : alk. paper) — ISBN 0-7914-4648-4
    (pbk. : alk. paper)
       1. Jesus Christ—Person and offices. I. Title.

BT202 .G695 2000
232—dc21
                                                                    99-050134

10 9 8 7 6 5 4 3 2 1

for Pat

CONTENTS

PREFACE

The world in which we live today is supposedly a secular one. Yet that world is full of Christs. The discussion that follows will confront us with Christ as liberator, the New Age Christ, black Christs, the cosmic Christ, and many other Christs besides. This potentially overwhelming pluralism presents a challenge to contemporary devotees of Jesus Christ. How can we sort through such apparent christological chaos?

The very assumption that the sorting process is worthwhile already locates this book between what I take to be two extremes. On the one side, there is the insular, dogmatic extreme. For proponents of that position, only one Christ can be valid, namely, my Christ, or the Christ embraced by my particular portion of the church. The other extreme is occupied by those who wish to make no distinctions at all: one Christ is as good as another. We are left, in that case, with an uncritical christological relativism.

The following pages attempt to find a way between these two extreme positions. It ought to be possible to make informed interpretive judgments about some of the many Christs offered for religious consumption, even to the extent of rejecting some of them. At the same time, it is surely possible to affirm the basic phenomenon of christological pluralism, perhaps even to the point of devoting oneself to more than one version of the Christ.

Chapter 1 lays the groundwork for our discussion by briefly considering the distinction between historical Jesuses on the one hand and Christs of faith on the other. We shall encounter a potentially bewildering pluralism in both cases. The chapter goes on to explore the notion of "imaginary Christs," a concept that will be crucial for understanding christological pluralism. Imagination is the creative, constructive element in thought. All of our thinking about the world involves some degree of imaginative construction. Where Christs of faith are concerned, however, imagination is an unusually important ingredient. The cognitive tools we use to grasp the ordinary world must be imaginatively stretched in order to approach the notion of the infinite God manifesting Godself in the form of the Christ. "Imaginary Christs" are not unreal Christs, then, but the constructions through which faith imaginatively approaches the reality of Jesus as the Christ.

It is the task of the second chapter to explain just how Christs of faith are rooted in the Christian tradition and its various subtraditions. This entails a consideration of how pluralism has informed the Christian tradition through its long history, and how it exercises a particularly strong influence on that tradition today. The last section of the chapter takes issue with currently popular interpretations of Christian tradition that picture it as a closed world of meaning, incommensurable with other worldviews. Acknowledging the all-important role of pluralism within the Christian tradition today necessitates understanding that tradition not as a religious ghetto, but as a collection of subtraditions open to one another and to various currents in the larger culture. The thoroughgoing interpenetration of the various subtraditions of Christianity means that the whole project of this book, the task of sorting through a plethora of Christs, should be undertaken not from a narrowly confessional perspective, but from the vantage point of the larger, ecumenical Christian tradition. And the Christian tradition's openness to the cultures around it suggests that the Christs whom we confront will often be affected by those cultures.

Chapter 3 proposes some specific criteria for testing Christs of faith. It begins with three venerable principles: First, a Christ of faith should bear a clear family resemblance to the Christs of the New Testament. Second, any Christ of faith should address the contention that the Christ is the presence of God. And, finally, every Christ must address the expectation that the Christ provides redemption. Chapter 3 asks how each of these criteria might help us sort through the multitude of christological claimants, and it investigates the pluralism that is internal to these criteria themselves.

Chapter 4 provides a concrete illustration of how an individual subtradition of the Christian faith can act back upon the larger Christian tradition, challenging it to make room for new Christs. The black Christs set forth by James Cone and Jacquelyn Grant are interpreted as powerful challenges to the Christs of the white American church. Indeed, the juxtaposition of white Christs with black Christs leads us to a critique of the former that charges them with "constitutive incompleteness."

Finally, chapter 5 briefly considers three questions that arise out of the exploration of christological pluralism undertaken in the preceding chapters: First, can one actually devote oneself to more than one Christ at a time? Second, can a Christian embrace another redeemer, such as the Buddha, in addition to the Christ? Third, can one who stands outside any religious tradition nonetheless draw upon religious traditions in order authentically to appropriate figures such as the Christ and the Buddha?

My sincere thanks to Dennis Bielfeldt and Steve Gowler, each of whom carefully read an early version of this book and, as is their habit, offered thoughtful and instructive comments on it. Thanks go too to my Religious Studies colleagues at Sacred Heart University: Walter Brooks, Anthony Cernera, Christel Manning, and Brian Stiltner. They are wonderful conversation partners, an essential stimulus for undertaking any worthwhile research project. A sabbatical leave awarded by Sacred Heart University was another crucial element making possible the completion of this book. Finally, I benefited a great deal from the comments of anonymous readers of the book manuscript.

CHAPTER 1

Historical Jesuses
and Imaginary Christs

From the very beginning of the Christian movement, there have been many Christs. Biblical scholars comment endlessly, for example, on the different titles used by the authors of the New Testament in their attempt to identify who Jesus of Nazareth really is. In addition to "Christ," which is itself a title, the New Testament applies to Jesus the titles "Son of Man," "Son of God," "Word," "Lord," "God," and "Emmanuel," among others.[1] Each of these can, in turn, be understood in various ways. Of course, these titles are not necessarily all at odds with one another. Especially since it is a transcendent reality that the New Testament authors claim to have in view, it should not be surprising that they find it necessary to employ numerous titles and descriptions; no one formulation can capture something that outstrips the finite reality in which all of our language is rooted. At the same time, the christological controversies of Christianity's first five centuries show a church struggling with genuinely different interpretations of the person and nature of Jesus Christ. The pronouncements of the great ecumenical councils such as Nicea and Chalcedon attempted to bring order to the church's faith about Christ, but as the eminent church father Athanasius recognized about Nicea, such pronouncements had the relatively modest goal of determining what could *not* be said about Jesus Christ. In other words, they merely set negative boundaries for the church's faith and teaching. Plenty of room remained for different positive formulations about the Christ, and this christological elbowroom has been thoroughly exploited down through the ages of Christian history. Many versions of Christ have found their way into Christian life and practice.[2]

This christological pluralism has continued unabated in our own time. In fact, as we shall see in chapter 2, there are a number of factors affecting modern Western Christianity—from the loss of authority of classic dogmatic pronouncements to the general pluralism of contemporary Western culture—that virtually guarantee our era an unprecedented number of Christs. What is more, these different Christs are not simply a function of there being different churches or Christian denominations.

Rather, the many Christs now often exist side by side within single churches, indeed within single congregations. Even a brief survey of some of the Christs that can claim followers today provides a striking sense of the potentially overwhelming pluralism of the contemporary scene.

We can begin with Jesus Christ as ethical teacher. There are many Christians today who, if asked for a summary of the essence of Christian faith, would reply with "Love your neighbor as yourself." While concern about the moral teachings of Jesus has obviously been a constant in Christian history, the tendency to focus on them in relative isolation from the more doctrinal strands of Christian tradition is a contemporary legacy of various movements in modern Western Christianity. The Enlightenment and Deism, for example, left their mark on American thought via figures such as Thomas Jefferson. And what came to be known as Protestant liberalism, a nineteenth-century movement in Protestant theology that was generally suspicious of traditional metaphysical and doctrinal formulations, continues to exercise influence on the theological agenda of mainline Protestantism in America. Nor should we overlook the impact of what is often labeled the "civil religion."[3] The civil religion is a set of public religious sensibilities and practices, usually purged of the specific tenets of individual religious traditions, that provides a background of piety for American society as a whole. It is displayed, for instance, in the obligatory references to God in presidential speeches, as well as in certain quasi-religious holidays such as Thanksgiving. Although the civil religion is ordinarily regarded as a watered-down version of the particular faiths that various Americans embrace, it also acts back upon those particular pieties. In its focus upon general ethical principles, backed up by only the vaguest of theological tenets, the civil religion reinforces a reading of Jesus Christ as first and foremost an ethical teacher.

Any survey of the ways in which contemporary Christians envision Christ must mention Christ as liberator. With intellectual support from Latin American liberation theology, as well as from feminist and African-American theologies, numerous Christians see Christ as the one who liberates the oppressed and leads the struggle against unjust practices and structures in society. Martin Luther King Jr. and Archbishop Romero of El Salvador provide dramatic models of devotion to Christ as liberator. Both men were martyred as a result of applying their vision of Christ as liberator to their respective societies. All versions of liberation christology attempt to persuade Christians that the Christ is directly relevant to the social and political orders of the world.

A seemingly very different version of Christ is offered by those who put him forth as a model of psychological well-being and a source of personal success. This very American version of Christ has been championed by a host of twentieth-century religious salesman. He was presented in the first third of the century by Bruce Barton's *The Man Nobody Knows*, which saw Jesus as a model of the successful business executive. The book's epigraph uses italics to give an unusual meaning to a familiar biblical passage—"Wist ye not that I must be about my Father's *business*?"—and it has chapters on Christ as "The Executive," "His Advertisements," and as "The Founder of Modern Business."[4] This sort of Christ received its most famous mid-century presentation in Norman Vincent Peale's *The Power of Positive Thinking*.[5] That this Christ is still popular today should come as no surprise, given our current appetite for self-help programs. One thinks here of Robert Schuller's "Hour of Power" Sunday-morning television broadcasts, beamed to thousands of homes from his Crystal Cathedral in California. Schuller's "possibility thinking" echoes Peale's earlier prescription for well-being.

If the image of Christ as a model of personal success is a fairly recent arrival on the scene, so also is the melding of Christ with so-called New Age spirituality. This Christ too is focused much more on the individual psyche and its quest for personal fulfillment than on the larger structures of society. A salient feature of the New Age movement is its internal pluralism. That is, in addition to its being one tendency among others within a pluralistic milieu, the New Age is itself built on the premise that one can borrow different insights from many times and places and put them together in an idiosyncratic designer spirituality. Thus, if Jesus Christ is to be made sufficiently malleable to serve as a resource for the New Age project, he must somehow be set free from his original context, not only in first-century Palestine, but also and especially from the tradition of the church. It is not surprising, then, that one finds on New Age bookshelves works such as *The Lost Teachings of Jesus*, by Mark L. Prophet and Elizabeth Clare Prophet.[6] The first part of that endeavor is titled "Missing Texts: Karma and Reincarnation," which suggests the way in which the authors want to associate Jesus with ideas different from those that hold sway in the Christian tradition. Similarly, the well-stocked New Age bookstore will have a copy of *Edgar Cayce's Story of Jesus*, which collects teachings about Jesus that Cayce derived from his clairvoyant readings.[7] Alongside these twentieth-century works, one may well find texts on something like the ancient gnostics, since Christian gnosticism is one of the first examples of the attempt to set forth a Christ who is in many ways different from the Christ championed by what turned out to be orthodox Christianity.[8]

While New Age spirituality draws on various currents that are sometimes loosely called "mystical," classical mysticism, the attempt to attain an unmediated relation to God, is garnering new interest in Amer-

ican society as well. College courses that treat Christian mystics from
John of the Cross to Julian of Norwich and that introduce students to
the Muslim Sufis and the Jewish Kabbalah are fully subscribed. Whatever the reason for this current interest, whether it be a passing fancy or
a heartfelt response to the perceived barrenness of the contemporary
spiritual landscape, it is inevitable that such an interest will help fuel a
Christ-mysticism. Christ as the object of mystical longing, as the "bride-
groom of the soul," an image drawn from the allegorical reading of the
biblical "Song of Songs," has a long and distinguished history within
Christian piety.[9] This Christ is reclaiming a place today, alongside the
other versions of the Christ.

The cosmic Christ too seems to have renewed relevance. "Cosmic
Christ" is the expression frequently used to designate the notion of
Christ as the Logos through which the universe was created and which
gives it its rational structure.[10] While Christ as model of psychological
wellbeing and the New Age Christ are both tightly focused on the individual, the cosmic Christ widens the believer's horizons to the boundaries of the very universe itself. At the same time, in its philosophical
abstraction from concrete human events, this model of Christ can be as
apolitical as its self-help and New Age counterparts. But we may well
find a new wrinkle in the idea of the cosmic Christ in our time, not only
insofar as it can be brought into discussion with the contemporary scientific conceptions of the universe—one thinks of Teilhard de Chardin's
finally unsuccessful attempts in this regard—but also thanks to present-
day ecological sensibilities. Christians seeking to find resources in their
faith for caring for the earth, and even for imbuing it with the character
of the sacred, have an ally in the cosmic Christ.[11]

Of current interest too is what, for want of a better term, I shall call
the Buddhist Christ. Given the genuine fascination on the part of many
Westerners, including Western Christians, with the religious traditions
of Asia, it is unsurprising that there are persons who approach the
Christ with spiritual sensibilities imbibed from the reading of Hindu,
Buddhist, and Taoist religious writings. A particularly striking example
is Stephen Mitchell's *The Gospel According to Jesus*, which brings to its
interpretation of Christ a wealth of knowledge on the great Asian traditions, and which tends to see Christ as a Zen master.[12]

Lest all of the Christs we have listed thus far seem somehow lacking in severity, it should be noted that the apocalyptic Christ has by no
means faded from the scene. Indeed, the Christian fundamentalism
invented in the modern West put new emphasis on this Christ and on
the murky passages in the book of Revelation that prophesy his advent.
In the latter half of the twentieth century, for example, the Cold War
between the Soviet Union and the United States provided ample fuel for

the apocalyptic fire: fundamentalist authors filled bookshelves and crowded lecture circuits with detailed explanations of how the prophecies of Revelation applied to Communist Russia, which these commentators identified with the Beast mentioned in Revelation, and how Armageddon would soon explode in the Middle East. The end of the Cold War did not, of course, spell the end of Christian apocalyptic expectations, anymore than did the passing of the many conditions in earlier Christian history that had been read through the lens of the book of Revelation. Furthermore, the change of the millennium has provided more than enough impetus for continued apocalyptic fervor among some Christians.

Finally, that Christ is present also who saves us from sin through the shedding of his blood on the cross. One might be tempted to call this the most traditional of the models of Christ that have contemporary appeal—has he not always been at the center of the Roman Catholic Mass, for instance?—were it not for the way in which this Christ too has been modified by modern American culture, especially by the individualism and the experiential emphasis of American piety. That this Christ has an important place among the many Christs that occupy our pluralistic scene is evidenced, first of all, by the powerful presence of evangelical Christianity in American society. The Christ who died to save the individual from his or her sins is still the preeminent version of Christ in evangelicalism. Billy Graham, despite his failing health, managed to continue preaching this Christ to millions of listeners right up to the end of the century. We can even add to the evidence for this Christ's popularity the incongruous but now familiar sight of fans at professional football games unfurling large, hand-printed banners marked "John 3:16."[13]

In the chapters that follow we shall have the opportunity to consider several approaches to Christ in more detail. But suffice it to say now, by way of introduction, that a worship service in the contemporary parish may find persons kneeling next to one another who are devoted to significantly different Christs. A number of caveats are in order, however, here at the outset.

First, the nine Christs we have briefly surveyed by no means exhaust the possible versions of Christ that are effective in contemporary Christianity. They simply represent some of the most familiar christological options of the day.

Second, the Christs of interest in our exploration of christological pluralism are those that are genuine options for ordinary Christians. While we shall touch on the ruminations of various theologians in order to plumb the implications of this pluralism, we shall not focus on the particular christologies of individual theologians for their own sake. In other words, the pluralism at issue here is not the many different Christs set forth in the contemporary christologies of professional theologians, but the diverse Christs operative in everyday Christian piety.

Third, the way in which the nine contemporary Christs have been described above, the manner in which they have been picked out and distinguished from one another, is inevitably artificial. In reality, the different approaches to Christ often overlap; their boundaries are not always as sharply drawn as our survey might suggest.

Fourth, and most important, is the fact that these Christs may well be *different* from one another without necessarily being *contradictory*. While there is little doubt that it is impossible to harmonize all of them, might it not be possible to find ways to fit some of them together, or at least to have them work peaceably side by side? This brings us to the central issues of the chapters that follow: How can we find our way among this confusing display of so many Christs? Is it possible, and is it legitimate, to look for the "genuine" Christ among this host of contenders? Should we look, instead, for genuine Christs? Or, in the end, must we be content with a veritable chaos of Christs, with no ordering principles available to us? Before we can begin our attempt to answer these questions in earnest, we must explore some crucial background categories and issues, culminating with the notion of "imaginary Christs."

We can begin our background work with a brief consideration of the modern distinction between the Jesus of history and the Christ of faith. By the phrase "the historical Jesus," or "the Jesus of history," scholars have usually intended that which can be known about the man Jesus of Nazareth simply via modern principles of historical research. The "Christ of faith," by contrast, is Jesus Christ as he is received and proclaimed in the church's attitude of faith and commitment. In theory, historical research should be able to provide us with an account of the actions and statements of Jesus. The transcendent dimension of reality, on the other hand, is beyond the purview of any empirical historical method. Christ in his divinity and as the risen Lord can only be grasped by faith. With the advent of modern historical methods of investigation in the eighteenth and nineteenth centuries, the question inevitably arose whether it is possible to escape christological pluralism by determining which version of the Christ of faith best complements the historical Jesus. This search for the historical Jesus undoubtedly owes much of its original impetus to modernity's disdain for what it regarded as the unsavory, because irrational, elements of Christian supernaturalism. But a related issue is surely the desire to avoid the destructive side of christological pluralism: European history with its wars of religion had shown Christians to be all-too-willing to do battle over their competing versions of Christ.

The beginnings of the quest for the historical Jesus can be dated with the posthumous publication of a manuscript fragment by the German scholar Hermann Samuel Reimarus in 1778.[14] Reimarus argued provocatively that the actual Jesus of history bore little resemblance to any version of Christ that could be preached by the church. Rather than being the same person approached from two different perspectives, the Jesus of history and the Christ of faith are, for Reimarus, wholly different figures. Reimarus' historical Jesus had expected to become a this-worldly, political messiah, but had died in despair. Belief in his resurrection was made possible by his disciples stealing his body from the tomb. But many writers who came after Reimarus, particularly in the nineteenth century, were convinced that research on the historical Jesus need not be used to undermine Christian commitment but could support it instead, even if the commitment that resulted involved a significant reworking of the church's traditional approach to Christ. As W. Barnes Tatum explains:

> The nineteenth century saw the rise of that theological movement known as Protestant "liberalism." . . . Liberal theologians desired a firm foundation for Christian belief and practice. They sought that foundation neither in the traditional creeds nor in the New Testament generally nor in the Gospels. Rather, they sought that foundation in the personality and religion of Jesus himself. Liberal theology emphasized Jesus not so much as savior but as teacher and example. It stressed not so much faith *in* but the faith *of* Jesus as he taught the Fatherhood of God and the brotherhood of humanity.[15]

In the case of Protestant liberalism, then, the discovery of the Jesus of history may not show us which Christ of faith is the correct one, since it prefers the faith of Jesus to faith in him, but it promises to perform a related task: it purports to show us how the very notion of Christian faith should be focused on the teaching of the man Jesus in a way that can eliminate the specter of warfare among competing dogmatic Christs. Partly as a result of this optimistic attitude about what historical research could do for Christian commitment, the "life of Christ" became a familiar genre in the nineteenth century.

The confidence displayed by the nineteenth-century biographers of Jesus suffered a serious blow at the beginning of the next century, a blow delivered by Albert Schweitzer's famous book *The Quest of the Historical Jesus*, which was published in Germany in 1906.[16] Schweitzer made it clear that most of the nineteenth-century attempts to write a historically accurate biography of Jesus were anything but objective historical efforts. Instead, the authors usually projected their own contemporary cultural sensibilities upon the figure of Jesus and recreated him in their own image. The real Jesus, argued Schweitzer, was not Protestant liber-alism's gentle ethical sage, but an apocalyptic prophet who mistakenly expected that he would bring in the Kingdom of God. Schweitzer's ver-sion of the historical Jesus bore little resemblance, then, to either the Jesus of the Protestant liberal biographers or the Christs preached by the churches.

In the wake of Schweitzer's book, and with a mounting skepticism about the Gospels' usefulness as historical records, the majority of Christian scholars in the first half of the twentieth century regarded the quest for the historical Jesus as pointless. The Gospels, they concluded, are not historical accounts from which it is possible to reconstruct a biography of Jesus. Rather, they are already testimonies of faith. Fur-thermore, anything that might be learned about the Jesus of history would be irrelevant to the Christ of faith. While the two need not be understood as antithetical in the way that critics such as Reimarus, and to a lesser extent Schweitzer, had suggested, the Christ of faith can exist very well on his own, independently of whatever paltry details about the historical Jesus might be available.

In recent years, however, there has been a resurgence of interest in the Jesus of history. Numerous books have appeared on the subject, and scholarly conferences on the historical Jesus have attracted wide atten-tion.[17] But the latest questers for the historical Jesus do not intend to embrace the naive assumptions of their forebears of the eighteenth, and especially the nineteenth, century. They continue to maintain, for exam-ple, that the Gospels do not provide the basis for a biography of Jesus. But they hold that the development of tools not utilized by biblical scholars in the past, tools provided by disciplines such as sociology and the history of religions, may be able to give us new insights into the social, cultural, and religious context in which Jesus of Nazareth lived and in terms of which he set forth his message. In addition, many of them are willing to countenance some relevance of the Jesus of history for the Christ of faith.[18] The depth of this recent Jesus research is often impressive, and the results deserve serious consideration by everyone from biblical scholars and theologians to laypersons. But on one partic-ular issue the latest version of the quest for the historical Jesus does not provide much help: anyone who looks to the results of this new quest for a quick escape from the dilemma of christological pluralism, if dilemma it be, will end up being sorely disappointed. For, as it turns out, there is pluralism here too. When we examine the work of some of the best-known participants in the new quest, we discover that the histori-cal Jesus set forth by Marcus Borg, for example, does not seem to be the same person as the one described by John Dominic Crossan, and Crossan's Jesus, in turn, seems a stranger to the man described by Ray-

mond Brown.[19] Crossan himself remarks on "the number of competent
and even eminent scholars producing pictures of Jesus at wide variance
with one another."[20] Furthermore, he suggests that this diversity is not
simply a contingent fact about the current crop of studies of the historical Jesus, but that it is inevitable. Because we have no direct access to
the Jesus of history, every so-called "historical Jesus" is in fact one possible reconstruction, one *reading of* the Jesus of history.[21] Each such
reading will be done from its author's particular vantage point. On the
surface, this observation is merely a hermeneutical truism: our age takes
it for granted that every historical reconstruction is perspectival. But the
observation takes on greater significance if we recall how few details we
have about the life of Jesus and how far removed we are from him in
time. While a reconstruction of the life of Frederick Douglass, for example, would necessarily be only one possible reading of him, it is highly
unlikely that it could support the degree of authorial creativity that any
historical reconstruction of the life of Jesus must bear. In any case, if the
quest for the historical Jesus was originally motivated, in part, by the
desire to escape from a potentially destructive christological pluralism,
it has not in fact provided any such escape. On the contrary, it simply
provides a new pluralism of its own; it offers us a host of historical
Jesuses.

While historians and others may have entertained the notion of flee-
ing from the many Christs of faith to the Jesus of history, numerous
twentieth-century Christian theologians have counseled Christians to
move in exactly the opposite direction. The issue for these theologians is
the potential danger of making faith beholden to historical research.
Must one wait to make a decision about Christian faith until the historians clear up certain ambiguities in the life story of Jesus, for example?
Should the believer alter his or her faith from day to day as the historians hem and haw, putting forth one conclusion and then quickly replac-
ing it with another? Could historical Jesus research ever come up with
evidence that would devastate the very foundations of Christian faith?
Many modern and contemporary theologians have understandably concluded that it is best to avoid these difficulties by seeing the Christ of
faith as largely independent of the results of historical research about
Jesus. They have sought, as Paul Tillich puts it in his comments on Martin Kähler's classic theological manifesto of 1896, to "make the certainty
of faith independent of the unavoidable incertitudes of historical
research."[22] Kähler himself speaks of finding an "invulnerable area"
(*sturmfreies Gebiet*) for faith, safely removed from the uncertainties of
the historian's trade.[23] Kähler has no doubt that the Christ of faith is a
response to the real historical individual, Jesus of Nazareth. But he holds
that we will never get to that individual, not to mention his larger sig-

nificance for our lives, by means of historical research.

For such influential followers of Kähler's position as Paul Tillich and Rudolf Bultmann, it makes little difference what one can or cannot know about the Jesus of history. All that is required for Christian faith is what Tillich, echoing Kahler, calls the "biblical picture" of Jesus as the Christ.[24] Nor are things entirely different for a more decidedly "neo-orthodox" theologian such as Karl Barth. This is not to say that Barth's Jesus is ahistorical. Barth would be loath to present Jesus Christ as merely an illustration of universal moral principles, for example, in the way that philosophers such as Immanuel Kant have done. The point, rather, is that the concrete figure of Jesus the Christ is encountered, for Barth, not via historical research but in the faithful witness of the Scriptures and the church.

While the work of Edward Schillebeeckx might be cited as an exception, most contemporary Roman Catholic theology also seems to relegate the quest for the historical Jesus to the background.[25] Karl Rahner's approach to christology via a transcendental and transcendent anthropology, for example, presents us with something much more akin to the Christ of faith than to the Jesus of history.[26] For Catholic thinkers, of course, Christ has always been encountered primarily through the Scriptures and the tradition of the church, not through historical research. Indeed, the contemporary catechism holds that the resurrected Lord is present to the faithful in the church in a more direct and powerful fashion than the man Jesus was to persons who encountered him as a historical individual in the first century:

> When his visible presence was taken from them, Jesus did not leave his disciples orphans. He promised to remain with them until the end of time; he sent them his Spirit. As a result communion with Jesus has become, in a way, more intense: "By communicating his Spirit, Christ mystically constitutes as his body those brothers of his who are called together from every nation."[27]

Of course the Christ of faith, the Christ experienced as present in the church in every age, should not be understood as somehow antithetical to the Jesus of history. While the Christ of faith is grasped through existential commitment rather than discerned via application of the modern historical method, the Christ of faith points to the same Jesus that historians attempt to describe. That is, while believers approach Jesus of Nazareth through the interpretive categories of faith, those categories are meant to be applied to the actual man Jesus, however difficult it may be to accumulate mundane, historical details about him. The Christ of faith, then, always makes reference to the historical individual, Jesus of Nazareth.

To summarize our explorations up to this point: christological pluralism is in full flower within contemporary Christianity. One might
suppose that some order could be brought to potential christological
chaos by going back to the historical Jesus and determining which ones
of the many Christs of faith are closest to the Jesus of history. But, whatever its other benefits, the quest for the historical Jesus proves to be of
little help in this regard. First, there is reason for skepticism about our
ability ever to recover significant information about the historical Jesus.
Second, the present state of the quest presents us with innumerable
Jesuses; pluralism simply reappears in another form. One cannot flee the
intimidating conflict and manyness of Christs of faith for the security of
an empirically certain Jesus of history. But numerous twentieth-century
Christian theologians have suggested proceeding the other way around:
we ought to flee the uncertainties of historical Jesus research for the existential and religious security of the Christ of faith. And thus we return
to the issue of christological pluralism. For now we must say to a Kähler or a Tillich, "Which Christ of faith ought I to embrace?" Perhaps it
is true that the most legitimate Christ of faith will be the one rooted in
the biblical picture of Jesus as the Christ. But is there only one such picture? It seems clear that the New Testament, which is the product of the
church's living and pluralistic tradition, contains many pictures of
Christ. And even if we were to agree to focus on just one of those pictures, would our interpretations of it coincide? That the New Testament
lends itself to a variety of interpretations is abundantly, and perhaps
frustratingly, clear to anyone having even the most cursory knowledge
of the Christian tradition.

All of this puts us in a position to consider the notion of imaginary
Christs. However much a particular version of the Christ of faith may
be a response to the actual historical individual, Jesus of Nazareth, and
however genuinely it refers to an eternal, transcendent Christ, human
imagination will forever play a crucial part in the generation of Christs
of faith. I use the word "imagination" here to refer to the creative, constructive element in human thought. All experience and knowledge
involve some degree of imagination. Even the most empirically derived
piece of scientific data entails a modicum of interpretation. Knowledge,
in other words, is never a merely passive affair. As philosophers from
Kant up to the present day have shown us, the mind cannot simply mirror the reality round about it, but must to some degree construct that
reality. It is certainly true, however, that different kinds of experience
and understanding require different degrees of imaginative construction
on the part of the knower.[28] We can envision a continuum along which
it is possible to plot, from left to right, approaches to the world which
require an ever-higher proportion of imagination. Scientific data collec-

tion will be plotted toward the left, low end of the continuum, while Christs of faith must be placed toward the high end.[29]

The contemporary pluralism of Christs, the fact that many Christs coexist within single churches, is a powerful indicator of the role of imagination in the formation of Christs of faith. There is no one Christ of faith that all Christians embrace, but rather many Christs, each the result of a different imaginative or constructive vantage point. But this christological pluralism only adds further evidence to other, more basic reasons for acknowledging imagination's especially potent role in the formation of Christs of faith. These other considerations can be tied to three paradoxes that will surface at various points in the chapters that follow. We begin, logically enough, with the *christological paradox*. From Tertullian, the second-century church father, to Soren Kierkegaard and his heirs in contemporary Christian thought, Christian theologians have wondered at the paradox of the infinite God taking on flesh and living and dying among us as a finite human being. Thus Tertullian wrote,

> You will not be "wise" unless you become a "fool" to the world, by believing "the foolish things of God." . . . The Son of God was crucified; I am not ashamed because men must needs be ashamed of it. The Son of God died; it is by all means to be believed, because it is absurd. And He was buried and rose again; the fact is certain, because it is impossible.[30]

Kierkegaard calls the idea of the God-man the "absolute paradox."[31] The notion of the infinite God becoming a human being appears to be a category mistake, the mixing of two disparate categories of reality. Thus, it is akin to asking, "What color is Monday?" As a category mistake, which is one particular kind of paradox, the concept of the God-man cannot be grasped via any of our ordinary conceptual machinery. It requires a creative leap of imagination, the kind of distortion of our ordinary conceptuality represented, for example, by nonliteral modes of thought and communication. Hence we find Kierkegaard resorting to parables in his treatment of the Christ-event.[32]

Closely related to the christological paradox is what we shall call the *revelation paradox*. Theologians of a certain stripe might be tempted to use the concept of divine revelation to avoid the need to credit human imagination in the construction of Christs of faith. But the revelation paradox consists in the fact that no appeal to divine revelation can ever avoid a firm reliance upon purely human faculties. First of all, how are we to decide which of many alleged instances of revelation are genuine? The point is precisely that *we* must decide that instance "a" is divine revelation, while instance "b" is not. John Locke, good Enlightenment philosopher that he was, clearly understood how human reason must come into play in any reception of revelation. The immediate revelation of God would seem to provide the most secure kind of knowledge, said Locke, but "our assurance can be no greater than our knowledge is, that it *is* a revelation from God."[33] Revelation can never outrun the role of human reason. Applied to Christian faith in the God-man, this means that the christological paradox is not simply a given to which one must subsequently respond. Rather, Christians must decide that Jesus is God, and hence that he represents the paradox of the God-man.

But, secondly, even when we have decided that a particular event or message is a divine revelation, we are not yet done with our constructive work. We must still grasp the content of that revelation. Imagination is required just in order to lay the groundwork for this task. Before we can grasp the life and action of Jesus as revelatory of God, for instance, we must employ imagination to discern a meaningful pattern in the events of Jesus' life and action. This point can helpfully be underscored by making use of Hans Georg Gadamer's treatment of art. In his attempt to free Western thought from the constricted notion of knowledge that limits it to what can be obtained by the objectifying methods of the natural sciences, Gadamer turns to art. For Gadamer, the work of art is not merely a matter of subjective experience, but a source of truth about the world. If reality is defined as what is untransformed, then art is "the raising up of this reality into its truth."[34] The work of art configures a confusing and disparate reality in such a way that we can grasp its true significance or essence. There is a sense, then, in which the artwork is truer than the original that it represents.

John Macquarrie applies Gadamer's insight to the writing of a gospel, so that we can see the element of imagination required to uncover the significance of the Christ story:

> A gospel does resemble a work of art in the sense that it does not merely copy the original or offer a second version of it, but, dare we venture to say, exposes the essence of the original, so that there takes place the event of the recognition of truth, the setting forth in uncon-cealedness (*aletheia*) of the fundamental meaning and reality of the original? . . . a gospel is concerned (to use Gadamer's phrase) with the recognition of the essence. It achieves its aim by weaving together historical incidents, teachings and sayings, mythological ideas, legendary accretions, theological reflections into a unique kind of discourse.[35]

Macquarrie uses as a concrete example the account of the trial of Jesus found in the Gospel of John:

> If there had been a clerk of court and he had left us a transcript of the trial, it might have made us see it very differently from the account in

the Fourth Gospel. But the evangelist whom we call John, by what Bultmann calls "a remarkable interweaving of tradition and specifically Johannine narration," has dramatically presented the essential meaning as he perceived it and as we are enabled to perceive it—a reversal of the roles of Jesus and his his judges, so that Jesus emerges as the judge while the ecclesiastical and political establishments are put on trial and found wanting. It is a remarkable transfiguration of the facts, not a distortion but rather an exposure of the reality. This is not just analogous to a work of art—it is itself an art-work of genius.[36]

Imagination is employed here, indeed an artistic imagination, in order to discern a meaning in the events and is required even just to uncover what we might term the mundane significance of these events.

To subsequently grasp such events as a revelation of God requires yet another use of imagination and takes us back into the territory of the christological paradox. The manifestation of an infinite God must be grasped and expressed in the only categories available to us, namely, those provided by our own finite languages and concepts.[37] The absolute paradox of the infinite God taking on finite human flesh, the christological paradox, requires a creative leap of imagination on the part of human beings precisely because it is a paradox. But *any* revelation of a genuinely infinite reality, whether or not it involves the infinite actually becoming identified with something finite, would find our ordinary conceptual inventory wanting, formed as that inventory is by the encounter of our finite cognitive resources with the finite world of which we are a part.[38] Thus, we are forced to choose between a rigorous *via negativa*, content to say only what the divine is not, or an imaginative use of language that creatively stretches it beyond its usual capabilities. The Thomistic doctrine of the analogical use of language, which pushes language beyond its everyday, univocal function, provides a classical example of the attempt to pursue the latter, creative option. There are really two levels of imaginative construction involved here. First, our everyday language is the result of a language tradition's imaginative creation of categories for understanding reality. Second, we must now imaginatively stretch those everyday categories. This second step takes the construction of God-concepts and Christs of faith well beyond the level of imaginative construction required for most other concepts.

If human initiative is required to recognize something as a revelation, and if imaginative construction is tied up with grasping and communicating it in even the most general sense, imagination is certainly evident in the attempt to communicate the revelation of Christ *to a particular time and place.* Josef Geiselmann has pointed out, for example, that if the words of Christ are intended to be living revelation, then the tradition of the church "cannot really reproduce what Jesus once said 'literally,' because it is intended to be Jesus' word now, in the Church's situation as God has brought it about."[39] Revelation, in order to continue to function as revelation, must be applied to ever-new situations. The imaginative task here is to discern and articulate identity in difference: if the being and words of Christ are to retain their identity in a new context, they must be creatively reinterpreted. The identity must be preserved through the use of formulations different from those employed in the past.

The third paradox that we shall encounter in our exploration of imaginary Christs can be designated the *transcendence paradox*. This third paradox has to do not so much with why imagination is necessary where Christs are concerned, but, having granted that necessity, with the importance of being self-conscious about the imaginative character of our christological constructs. Christs of faith are about transcendence: they are meant to be apprehensions of Christ as the presence of God. Our preliminary investigation of the christological and revelation paradoxes has reinforced the familiar fact that the phenomenon of transcendence strains our finite faculties. The infinite, almost by definition, leaves those faculties behind, so that we are forced to fall back upon imagination in order to fill in the blanks in our knowledge of the divine, to respond to the "blank wonder" occasioned by the presence of the infinite.[40] The paradox presently at issue is that the most adequate response to such transcendence will be the one that most fully understands the *ina*dequacy of its finite categories. Nothing more often serves as a screen upon which to project our all-too-human prejudices, desires, and ambitions than our notions of divinity, as Feuerbach and Freud would be happy to remind us. A theology can confidently describe God's transcendence in the most exalted terms but still end up advancing a view of the divine that is almost wholly self-serving. Indeed, this very confidence in one's abilities to describe the divine transcendence is what most effectively blinds one to the phenomenon of projection. By contrast, then, a formulation that is self-conscious about its humanness may, paradoxically, be better able to communicate genuine transcendence. Modern theological programs that appear to keep the transcendence paradox in view include the dialectical theology paradigmatically expressed in Karl Barth's *Romans*, which attempts to maintain the dialectic of "yes" and "no" in all of our talk about God, and Paul Tillich's discussion of the self-negating religious symbol, where the symbol undoes its own finite content in its effort to point to the divine.[41]

Yet another factor to be considered in understanding the role of imagination in the construction of Christs of faith, and perhaps the factor that brings us into greatest proximity to our ordinary use of the word "imaginary," is the need for devotees of the Christ to imaginatively concretize and round out their pictures of him. Jesus as the Christ is understood not as an abstract version of God, but as the incarnation of God, that is, God in the concrete form of a particular human being. Christ provides access to God, so Christian faith claims, precisely insofar as Christ possesses this human concreteness. But the New Testament does not round out the person of the Christ for us. It is notoriously silent about matters such as the childhood of Jesus or his physical appearance, matters that would help us to grasp the concrete, personal reality of Jesus as the Christ. The pluralism of New Testament Christs is a factor here too, inasmuch as it means that the New Testament presents us with rough versions of many Christs, rather than with a fully realized version of one Christ of faith.

It is up to the individual believer, then, to imaginatively round out the personhood of Jesus as the Christ so as to be able to approach him as a concrete individual. The devotee of the cosmic Christ may picture a magisterial figure, for example, while the follower of Christ as liberator may imagine a volatile spokesman for and companion of the poor. It is unsurprising that artists carry out this imaginative task with particular effectiveness. A noteworthy contemporary example is provided by Pier Paolo Pasolini's 1964 film, *The Gospel According to St. Matthew*. While not a believer in any ordinary sense, Pasolini succeeds in bringing to life Jesus the Christ as a passionately committed, almost angry, religious seer who identifies with the poor. Pasolini follows the text of Matthew's gospel closely. He accomplishes his imaginative rounding out of Jesus as the Christ not by adding new events and new dialogue, but through the concrete presentation of what is already contained in the gospel: Pasolini has a particular actor, in a particular setting, give a particular interpretation of the words and deeds of Jesus.[42]

The average follower of Jesus as the Christ will probably not accomplish the kind of full-blown imaginative rounding out found in Pasolini's film. But some effort in that direction is required if the Christ is to be encountered as a concrete figure, the one intended in the Christian doctrine of the incarnation. This imaginative realization of the figure of the Christ does not entail any kind of psychobiography. It is not necessary to reconstruct the psychological development of Jesus of Nazareth, but only to imbue him with the concrete personhood required for one to encounter him as a specific individual.

It is worth noting how this imaginative rounding out of the figure of Jesus as the Christ, by its very act of individualizing the Christ, tends to differentiate Christs of faith from one another all the more powerfully. The genuine pluralism of Christs of faith becomes especially apparent, in other words, when the different pictures of the Christ are each imaginatively filled out so as to become concrete individuals.

Lest we lose sight of our central topic, it is necessary to recall at this point that the existence of a plethora of different Christs side-by-side in contemporary Christian piety powerfully reinforces the sense that Christs of faith are imaginative human responses to Jesus of Nazareth and the chain of events that he set in motion. My Christ is different from the Christ of the person worshipping next to me, in large part because of the imaginative, constructive component in the being of all Christs. After all, imagination, by its very nature, differs from one time and place to another, from one group to another, and even from one individual to another.

We have considered a number of reasons why this imaginative component is essential to Christs of faith. First, our language, which already bears an imaginative interpretation of everyday reality, must be imaginatively stretched in order to approach the paradox or category mistake of Christ being both God and man. Second, constructive work is required in order to judge that something qualifies as a revelation of God. Third, if we are to grasp the content of any such revelation, the ground must be prepared by finding meaningful order in a particular constellation of events. Gadamer's account of how the work of art raises reality up into its truth provides a model for this third instance of imaginative construction. Imagination comes into play, fourthly, in the actual event of grasping the content of the revelation, or of anything that transcends the finite. This again requires an imaginative stretching of our finite categories of thought and communication. Imagination is required, fifthly, in order to discern identity in difference, which in this case is a matter of deciding what the venerable figure of Jesus as the Christ has to say in each new time and place. Sixth, imagination is apparent in the act of rounding out the figure of the Christ so that one can approach him as the presence of God in a concrete individual, rather than as an abstract manifestation of God.[43]

Thus, while even our most mundane dealings with reality require some degree of imaginative interpretation, the creation of Christs of faith draws upon imagination to an unusually high degree. It is this fact that warrants the expression "imaginary Christs." At the same time, it should already be evident from what has been said above that the expression "imaginary Christs," as it is being used here, is in no way intended as synonymous with "unreal Christs." On the contrary, if there are any genuine Christs to be found, they will be functions of human imaginative construction in the ways that we have just indicated. Thus, Christian orthodoxy may judge a particular imaginary Christ, or several such Christs, an entirely proper response to the historical man, Jesus of Nazareth and to his transcendent reality as the risen Lord. Or, in terms of a less thoroughly orthodox perspective, the kind of perspective opened up by the nonmetaphysical interpretations of God that we shall touch on in chapter 3, an imaginary Christ or Christs may be deemed a genuine response to Jesus and to a real element of transcendence that Jesus uncovered in the relationship of human beings with their universe.

Of course, we ordinarily use the word "imaginary" to refer to a construction that does not correspond to anything in reality. Hence, we say that a unicorn is an "imaginary beast," for example. But note that we would find it odd to use the phrase "imaginary unicorns." This phrase strikes us as misguided not in that it is simply redundant, but inasmuch as it suggests that there must exist at least one real unicorn, if we are to pick out others as imaginary. The expression "imaginary Christs" implies, then, that there does exist a real Christ. But it also suggests that our approaches to the real Christ involve an unusually large amount of imaginative work. That is, while we do usually reserve the word "imaginary" for constructions that do not correspond to reality at all, that word is useful here as a self-conscious device to help us keep in view the role of imagination in our Christ-making. It is important to keep the imaginative component in Christ-making ever in sight, given the truth of the transcendence paradox: those approaches to the transcendent are most adequate that recognize the limitations, the humanness, of their own conceptual and linguistic tools.

Thus, Christs of faith are imaginary, in our use of the term, but not unreal. Far from equating imaginary Christs with unreal Christs, we need to ask questions such as the following: "Which of the many imaginary Christs of faith confronting contemporary Christians are genuine Christs?" "What does it mean to talk about a 'genuine' Christ or Christs in the first place?" "Is there any way to settle on criteria of 'reality' or 'genuineness' without falling into dogmatic presumptuousness?" "Should we expect to find as many criteria for genuineness as there are Christs?"

Perhaps these questions will make some persons uneasy. Surely christologial pluralism is to be celebrated rather than avoided. After all, no single imaginative construction can adequately grasp the reality of Jesus as the Christ. Thus, we get ever closer to that reality by putting together more and more perspectives on the Christ. The more vantage points upon which we are able to draw, the more profound will be our grasp of the reality of the Christ. Christological pluralism is advantageous too on a more mundane level: by allowing pluralism to flourish, we make it less likely that one particular version of the Christ will be invested with special authority and used as an instrument of power and coercion.

If christological pluralism is in fact to be prized rather than decried, why ask questions intended to sort out the various imaginary Christs of faith? Why not just revel in the plethora of Christs that the human imagination is able to concoct? Consider three answers to this understandable query. First, however much champions of a particular sort of postmodernist sensibility may attempt to dissuade us from pursuing questions of truth, those questions inevitably intrude in any serious and practical confrontation with the world. In the context of Christs of faith, truth itself may be construed pluralistically, of course. Your criteria for determining which Christ or Christs truly reflect Jesus of Nazareth as the Christ may legitimately be different from my criteria. But we can nonetheless both make sense out of the idea that some imaginary Christs may truly reflect the figure of Jesus and his role as manifestation of the divine, while other Christs may distort those things. For instance, feminist theologians will probably not have the same standards of truth in view in their evaluation of Christs as did Thomas Aquinas or Friedrich Schleiermacher or Karl Barth. Yet they will still have standards of truth, and they will most likely utilize them to reject as perversions of the real Jesus Christ any Christs of faith that support the oppression of women. Feminist theologians, in other words, have tended not to champion a normless pluralism, but to work toward a pluralism that avoids unjust and oppressive Christs.

Second, far from our proposed christological sorting process being a tyrannical undertaking intended to quash difference, some such process is required as part of our responsibility to other human beings. Religious commitment is a dangerous phenomenon. Human history is an all-too-shocking record of the sufferings human beings are prepared to impose upon one another in the name of religion, from crusades to inquisitions to campaigns of ethnic cleansing. Thus, it is imperative that we test the spirits before we endorse any religious perspective. One who wishes to embrace a Christ of faith is responsible for picking out of the vast number proposed for devotion a Christ or Christs who will engender, in however modest a fashion, a more humane world rather than a more ghastly one.

Third, the attempt to sort through the many Christs of faith that inhabit the contemporary scene and determine which ones of them are in some sense genuine is not tantamount to a rejection of christological pluralism. On the contrary, the assumption here is that many imaginary Christs will be deemed genuine. It should be possible, however, to reject *some* Christs. We ought not to be reduced to a mindless christological relativism. In order to avoid that fate and to understand how it might be possible meaningfully to sort through the many Christs of faith, we must begin with a consideration of the relation of christological pluralism to the Christian tradition. This we shall attempt to do in the next chapter.

CHAPTER 2

Tradition and Subtraditions

We have seen that, while there are good reasons for celebrating the pluralism of Christs, it is incumbent upon followers of Jesus as the Christ to engage in some kind of sorting process where imaginary Christs are concerned. The attempt must be made, however tentative and humble, to find the genuine Christs among the host of christological contenders. This quest for genuine Christs leads us inevitably to the classical Christian tradition, the tradition of the great ecumenical councils, for example, that have formed the sensibilities of Eastern Orthodox, Roman Catholic, and mainline Protestant Christianity over the bulk of Christian history. It must be emphasized from the outset, however, that this alignment with the Christian tradition does not imply adherence to one rigid interpretation of that tradition, not even on some of the most fundamental ontological issues. For instance, our later exploration of what we shall call nonprovidential Christs will take us outside traditional notions of God and transcendence. What is more, the Christian tradition must be open to new interpretation if it is to overcome the injustices that have been part of its history. Jacquelyn Grant reminds us of the feminist conviction, for example, that "appeals to tradition in mainstream male articulated theologies often have been nothing more than a way of reinforcing male patriarchal history."[1] And, as Grant herself is quick to add, such appeals have repeatedly been used to the detriment of minority populations and of the poor. But we nonetheless need to steer by the tradition in some fashion. Why is this so?

We need to orient ourselves by the Christian tradition *in order to secure an objective identity for Christs of faith.* The attempt to show that this is the case begins with a more precise analysis of what is meant by the Christ of faith. Let us specify that the Christ of faith, in its most venerable guise, is (1) the man Jesus (2) received in the attitude of faith as (3) the presence of God. We can take the parts in turn and consider the extent to which each is dependent upon the Christian tradition.

Surely one can seek the first component, the historical Jesus, without orienting oneself by the commitments of the Christian tradition. It is of course true that the only documents that provide us with significant information about Jesus are already religious testimonies. The New Testament is itself a product of the early Christian tradition; it is, as the saying goes, the church's book. But there are other gospels, the Gospels of Thomas and Peter, for example, that were rejected by that portion of the Christian tradition that later won the right to determine what would constitute Christian orthodoxy. Furthermore, one can choose to read the New Testament against the grain of the tradition that produced and sustained it. Many seekers of the historical Jesus over the past few centuries have thought that this is in fact the best way to find the real Jesus.

If we jump to the third element in our formula for construing the Christ of faith, that is, Christ as the presence of God, we enter an arena where it may again be possible to do without the Christian tradition, though the church itself has usually denied this. If the infinite God of traditional Christian theology exists, is the Christian tradition the only avenue to that God? The spokespersons of the church down through the ages have had internal theological reasons as well as political-ecclesiastical reasons for affirming that "outside the church there is no salvation." But surely there is no prima facie impossibility to the idea that one can get to God some other way. Of course, we have seen that there can be no direct access to the transcendent. Thus these other avenues to God would also have to involve a healthy dose of imaginative construction. But perhaps, to borrow the Hindu vocabulary, there is more than one avatar of the Godhead, so that there can be a Krishna of faith and a Shiva of faith, as well as a Christ of faith. Whatever may appear to be the case from within the Christian tradition, there does not seem to be any external necessity to turn to that tradition in order to seek God.

It is when we consider the middle term, which holds the formula together, that we encounter the necessity of orienting ourselves by the Christian tradition. For a Christ of faith is not simply the man Jesus, nor simply the presence of God, but the man Jesus received in an attitude of faith as the presence of God. But couldn't even such a Christ of faith be sought outside the Christian tradition? We have already suggested that it is possible to read the New Testament against the grain of the tradition that produced and sustained it. Could not one use the New Testament as a jumping off point for his or her own idiosyncratic brand of commitment to Jesus as the presence of the divine, a commitment that thoroughly rejected the pronouncements of bodies such as the Council of Nicea? The answer, of course, is that this is not only possible, but that it actually occurs. But there is nonetheless something crucial missing in this kind of traditionless, idiosyncratic Christ-formation. The Christian tradition is an invaluable testbed for Christs of faith. It consists of two millennia of experience in attempting to live out devotion to the Christ of faith. On the basis of this rich experience of what it means to attempt to live one's life focused on the Christ, it is possible to reject some interpretations of the Christ. Perhaps some of the nine Christs we briefly surveyed at the beginning of our first chapter, for example, eventually can be rejected on the basis of criteria that have emerged over the long haul of Christian experience with Christs of faith. Many Christs will still exist within the Christian tradition even after these criteria have been allowed to work. But these Christs will, in turn, constantly be juxtaposed to one another, both complementing and limiting one another.

It is just this process that secures something akin to an objective identity for Christs of faith, however many they be. The man Jesus, if he existed, had a definite, objective identity. The simplest and perhaps clearest element of this identity was, as with all human beings, his self-identical physical body: it is the same body (albeit one that maintains identity through the differences of constant growth and replenishment) that does one thing today and something else tomorrow. More profound forms of identity rest upon this physical foundation. But we have little or no access to the historical Jesus, and the Christ of faith is not simply identical to the Jesus of history in any case.

The transcendent God, if it is real, not only has an objective identity, but is the very ground of all objectivity and all identity. But, again, we can get at this God, if at all, only through imaginative constructions of faith.

Thus, we are back to Christs of faith. But how can Christs of faith, especially since they are multiple, have any objective identity? Can't they be constructed in just about any fashion? They have an identity precisely insofar as they are rooted in the Christian tradition, having thus, in effect, passed through the crucible of that tradition's centuries of practical, existential testing. *It is this rooting that allows us to say that a particular Christ, despite being one of many Christs rooted in the Christian tradition, ultimately points to the same reality meant by others who have used the expression "Christ" down through the ages.*

This need to orient ourselves by the Christian tradition in order to secure some degree of objective identity for Christs of faith illustrates Gadamer's contention that "to stand within a tradition does not limit the freedom of knowledge but makes it possible."[2] The Enlightenment, and those influenced by it down to the present day, tend to see tradition as blocking us from understanding events and persons of the past. They hold that the particular commitments of a tradition are dogmatic prejudices that blind us, so that we are not able to understand the past in its own terms. But this attitude is itself, in Gadamer's famous description, a prejudice: "The fundamental prejudice of the enlightenment [sic] is the prejudice against prejudice itself, which deprives tradition of its power."[3] There are, of course, countless illegitimate prejudices "which it is the undeniable task of the critical reason to overcome."[4] But the legitimate prejudices of a tradition make it possible for us to grasp a historical reality, not just as an isolated monad (which is a falsifying abstraction suggested by a certain reading of the scientific method), but as it has impressed itself upon later persons and events. This history of the reality's influence, which is held fast in the commitments of a tradition, is part of the very being of the thing. Thus, unless one is open to the historical reality's own effective history, one cannot grasp its significance. Put in terms of the present issue, unless one is open to the effect that the Christ of faith has had in the long experience of the Christian tradition, one will miss a crucial part of the reality of Christs of faith.

As a result of this need to orient our discussion of Christs of faith by the Christian tradition, the task that confronts us now is to consider how christological pluralism has challenged and continues to challenge that tradition. To this end, we shall consider three different forms of the struggle between Christian tradition and the phenomenon of many Christs. While, in reality, these three forms of that perennial struggle overlap with one another, we shall separate them artificially for purposes of clarity.

We begin with *different Christs appearing in different ages of a unified Christian tradition.* In other words, this first scenario involves the great tradition of Christianity, that larger tradition held together by the Scriptures and the ecumenical councils; we are not concerned in this instance with the many subdivisions of the tradition. Furthermore, we are bracketing here the fact that many Christs can exist within this one larger tradition at one and the same time. It is the appearance of different Christs through time within this one tradition that is at issue for us now.

It is undeniable that a Christ who appeals to one epoch of the Christian tradition may be unattractive to Christians of another time. Thus, the severe Christ Pantocrator, the cosmic ruler dispensing justice from his heavenly throne, may find himself replaced in the contemporary era by a Christ who empowers the individual person in the responsible use of his or her freedom. Christs do, to some extent at least, change with the times. Some of these changes may ultimately be rejected by the Christian tradition as merely the result of infatuation with the superficial sensibilities of a particular cultural moment. But even after that sifting process has taken place, we will probably still find Christ Pantocrator at one end of the timeline of Christian history and the Christ who empowers human freedom at the other.

The challenge for the tradition, then, is to discern how different Christs of faith that appear as Christian history unfolds are ultimately all the same Christ. There must be an underlying christological identity amidst the obvious differences. How can the particular Christs of faith that appear in different periods of Christian history be shown actually to possess an underlying unity? Because Christs of faith, precisely as products of faith, have a practical, existential focus, rather than a theoretical one, the church might try to discern identity in difference in functional terms here. Thus, in attempting to determine whether a present-day variation on Christ is genuine, interpreters of the Christian tradition might operate on the assumption that a genuine Christ is one that makes possible the same way of life that Christ made possible in this tradition in the past. The characteristic components of this way of life could include a particular kind of experience, of moral behavior, of relationships within the Christian community, and of redemption. Of course, to decide on a principle of discernment such as this one is only part of what is required, for the principle cannot simply be applied in mechanical fashion. One will have to ask how it is possible to determine that two experiences are the same, or two patterns of moral behavior, or of community, or of redemption. The kind of redemption effected by Christ as Pantocrator will surely not be identical in all respects to the sort provided by the Christ who empowers human freedom. But might they be identical on some more essential level? The task of finding identity in difference through the various epochs of the Christian tradition is never cut-and-dried; it is always a matter of interpretation, with all of its attendant risks and uncertainties.

No matter what strategy is adopted to find the identity among the differences in the various Christs that have appeared down through the centuries of Christian history, there is one principle of interpretation that will probably be common to them all. It is a principle that we shall call the christological circle. Thanks to the work of thinkers such as Schleiermacher and Heidegger, we are familiar with different versions of the hermeneutical circle. In the dialectic of part and whole, for example, I interpret a text or event by understanding certain individual parts as keys to the meaning of the whole, but as I proceed in this interpretation, my understanding of the whole acts back upon my understanding of the individual parts. Or, in the case of the Heideggarian notion of the forestructure of understanding, I must approach an interpretive task with a pre-understanding of what is to be grasped if I am to be able even to initiate that task. But, as understanding proceeds, my pre-understanding will be corrected or modified. The christological circle is another version of the hermeneutical circle.

We have seen that, while Christs of faith can arise outside the context of the Christian tradition, they have an essential relationship to that tradition. Yet it is undeniable that the sensibilities of the particular societies and cultures in which the Christian tradition finds itself have a powerful influence on the creation and interpretation of Christs of faith.

We can think again at this point about the Christ who empowers the individual in his or her freedom. This Christ of faith would not exist, at least in his present form, were it not for the emphasis in modern and postmodern Western society on individual autonomy. It is a notorious fact that earliest Christianity, far from identifying the life of Christian faith with freedom in our sense, took for granted the institution of slavery. Thus, in his epistle to Philemon, the apostle Paul explains that he is returning the escaped slave Onesimus to his master. Although it is clear that Paul would like Onesimus as a particular individual to be treated as a brother in Christ rather than as a slave, Paul gives no indication that he opposes slavery as an institution.[5] And later Christianity tolerated centuries of slavery, even in those societies supposedly directly informed by Christian principles.[6] The fact that abolitionist sentiments do not appear with any frequency within Christian circles until the late seventeenth century reinforces the sense that it took the strong currents of modernity, brimming with concerns about individual dignity and rights, to finally sweep away the institution of slavery. Today, it would be hard to find a Christian who did not regard slavery as antithetical to the very meaning of Christian faith (though, until very recently, many South African Christians apparently saw no conflict between Christ and apartheid). It is clear, in other words, that the mores of the surrounding culture have altered how Christians imagine Christ.

But this influence of a host society and culture upon the tradition's perception of its Christs does not exhaust the dynamic at work here. For, to stay with the same example, Christians will now go back to their notions of Christ in order to come to a more profound grasp of the meaning of individual freedom. That is, societal and cultural forces reshape Christs of faith with concerns about human autonomy, but Christians return to those Christs, convinced that true human freedom was to be found there all along and that Christian faith ultimately provides a deeper perspective on that freedom than modern and postmodern culture afford. We find a concrete example of this cycle of interpretation in Pope John Paul II's encyclical on the contemporary moral scene, *Veritatis Splendor* (The Splendor of Truth). The pope begins with an acknowledgment of the way in which modern Western culture has contributed to our awareness of the importance of human freedom: "Certainly people today have a particularly strong sense of freedom."[7] The right to religious freedom and the respect for conscience are, says the pope, increasingly understood as "the foundation of the cumulative rights of the person. This heightened sense of the dignity of the human person and of his or her uniqueness, and of the respect due to the journey of conscience, certainly represents one of the positive achievements of modern culture."[8] But the burden of his argument is to show how the

same modern culture that did us a service by highlighting human freedom and dignity often perverts the meaning of freedom. True freedom,
he thinks, can be found only through Christ.

This dialectic of interpretation is the christological circle, and it
informs the whole historical unfolding of the Christian tradition in its
interaction with various societies and cultures. The precise nature of that
interaction, and hence of the christological circle itself, will vary depend-
ing on the particular relationship of the tradition to the surrounding
social and political structures. The christological circle had a much
smaller circumference, as it were, in medieval Christendom than it has
in contemporary postmodern culture. But the circle is always operative
in some fashion, since the Christian tradition can never be sealed off
entirely from the world around it.

The second version of the tradition's struggle with christological
pluralism that we must explore is the phenomenon of *different subtraditions within the larger Christian tradition competing to define the
real Christ.* Let us describe the larger Christian tradition as the Bible and
the ecumenical councils, which are the common heritage of the subtraditions, plus the other tenets and practices that are held by all of the
subtraditions today. An example of a tenet held in common by at least
the vast majority of the subtraditions today that might not have been
held by them earlier, even though it is now regarded as following from
the Scriptures and ecumenical councils, is the aforementioned belief that
the Christ empowers individual autonomy.

While the notion of subtraditions can be used to describe various
groups and currents within the larger church, it applies most obviously
to the different churches resulting from the division of Christianity into
Eastern Orthodoxy, Roman Catholicism, and Protestantism. There are,
in turn, a host of subdivisions within Protestant Christianity, from
Lutheranism to the Baptist churches, and these can subdivide yet again,
so that in this country alone we have a number of different Lutheran
bodies, for example. Thanks to such denominational divisions, later
Christian history is powerfully influenced by a struggle among different
churches, each of which tends to suppose that it possesses the most adequate Christ or Christs of faith. It is clear that this struggle has often
been harmful to the overall health of Christianity. Even in the best of
times, it has fostered self-righteousness and parochialism; in the worst of
times it has resulted in outright warfare.

But there is another side to this story, for one can also see the competition among the various subtraditions within Christianity as providing a system of checks and balances that ultimately benefits the larger
tradition's production of Christs of faith. The Scriptures and ecumenical
councils are the common heritage of all of the major subtraditions. Each

subtradition will claim that its current version or versions of Christ faithfully mirror that heritage. But each subtradition's Christs are at least implicitly in a dialogue, however polemical, with the Christs of the other subtraditions. It seems plausible, then, that any Christ that deviates significantly from the common heritage of the larger Christian tradition will, in the end, effectively be shown wanting by the other subtraditions and, as a result, eventually either be withdrawn from competition or substantially modified.[9] For example, the extreme individualism supported by some American Protestant christologies in the past has always been under pressure from the classical emphasis on the Christian community found in Roman Catholicism, Lutheranism, Episcopalianism, and Eastern Orthodoxy, among other subtraditions. This extreme individualism is on full display, as Pelikan reminds us, in the words of a popular hymn describing a garden liaison with Jesus:

> I come to the garden alone,
> While the dew is still on the roses.
> And the voice I hear,
> Falling on my ear,
> The Son of God discloses.
> And He walks with me and He talks with me,
> And He tells me I am His own.
> And the joys we share, as we tarry there,
> *None other has ever known.*[10]

But the United Methodist Church, for example, whose forebears would have been quite comfortable with this hymn, has pulled back a good deal from such individualism in the last quarter of the twentieth century, as evidenced, to take but one example, in its greater contemporary emphasis on such corporate dimensions of church life as the liturgy and the celebration of Holy Communion. One can argue that this move away from an extraordinarily individualistic christology has much to do with the pressure exerted by the corporate emphasis in other subtraditions of the faith.

We have seen how the larger tradition can call into question an interpretation of the Christ of faith advanced by one of the subtraditions. But, of course, the individual subtraditions also act back upon the whole. The great Christian tradition is an abstraction; it is essentially the sum of the subtraditions that make it up, minus the practices and tenets that divide them. Thus, the changes that befall the tradition's Christs of faith—changes stimulated by internal theological exigencies, by the practical experience of Christians, by social and cultural forces, to name but a few factors—enter through individual subtraditions.

But we should note that there are two different ways in which the subtraditions might act back upon the tradition. Suppose, for example, that while the tradition limits the individualistic bent of a particular subtradition's Christ of faith, some of the subtradition's means of artistically communicating its faith end up influencing the larger tradition. This is a case in which the subtradition's action upon the tradition probably does not affect the substance of the larger tradition's christological tenets. But there is surely a second sort of situation, in which the subtradition's effect on the larger tradition does alter, however slightly, the substance of the tradition's christologies. For example, what might be called the liberationist subtradition of contemporary Christianity is presently having an important impact on the larger Christian tradition's sense of the Christ's relationship to the social and political dimensions of human life. To cite a specific instance, we shall see in chapter 4 that the Christ (or Christs) of African American liberation theology offers a potent challenge to American Christianity as a whole. And if this sort of dynamic is, as seems likely, a regular occurrence, then a significant interpretive movement is imparted to the whole interaction between tradition and subtraditions: the criteria applied by the larger tradition in its implicit judgment of the subtraditions undergo constant change. The larger tradition checks the extreme proposals of the individual subtraditions. And the individual subtraditions act back upon the larger tradition, subtly or dramatically changing it in turn. But this means that, to put it simplistically, the next time that the larger tradition applies its christological criteria in judgment of a Christ set forth in a particular subtradition, those criteria will be different from the ones the tradition wielded at an earlier time. The interpretive dynamic between the tradition and its subtraditions, then, is reminiscent of a ballerina pirouetting across the stage: she turns about her vertical axis—the reciprocal relationship of tradition and subtradition—while simultaneously traversing the length of the stage—the continual change in the whole tradition and the christological criteria that it brings to its dialogue with the subtraditions.

In taking this view of the matter, we have in effect put together our first two forms of the tradition's struggle with christological pluralism: we see the many Christs of the different subtraditions competing to define the genuine Christ, as well as the generation of new Christs in different epochs of the larger tradition as it unfolds in time. We have noted the constant interpretive movement here: it is not only Christs that change, but the criteria for evaluating them, since those criteria are themselves read off from contemporary Christs of faith. This continual evolution of the Christian tradition raises the question of an underlying essence or identity. Does the tradition, by changing even its criteria over time, eventually evolve into something wholly different from where it started? Does it, in other words, periodically change its inner being, its identity, over the long haul of Christian history? Or is there some underlying identity amidst the differences, so that the differences in fact serve to express that identity the more effectively in each new epoch? Christian thinkers of a reasonably traditional bent will, of course, opt for the latter scenario. They will hold that the constant interpretive movement characterizing the tradition is a matter of development, not of rupture with the tradition's origins. The guarantee of this for persons of a traditional kind of faith is the work of the Holy Spirit as the member of the Godhead who guides the tradition is its journey through time.[11]

This analysis of the tradition's confrontation with christological pluralism, both down through time and via numerous subtraditions existing simultaneously, puts us in a position to understand the third scenario that we must explore, that is, *the unprecedented number of Christs found within single subtraditions, or even single congregations, in contemporary Christianity.* We shall consider four different reasons for this historically unique degree of internal pluralism. First, perennial touchstones of christological orthodoxy such as the dictates of Nicea and Chalcedon have lost their authority in much of contemporary Christianity. This is true for numerous theologians as well as for laypersons within the churches. Theologians and philosophers of religion have been chafing for several centuries now under the burden of what some of them regard as the outmoded substantialist metaphysic of the church's early christological pronouncements. To speak as Nicea does, for instance, of Christ being "of one substance with the father," the famous *homoousios*, already bothered theologians such as Schleiermacher.[12] A more contemporary and strident dissatisfaction is expressed in a work such as *The Myth of God Incarnate*, a collection of articles by various British theologians.[13] But more significant than the philosophically motivated dissatisfaction of theologians is the simple absence of Nicea and Chalcedon in the background of lay consciousness. The Nicene Creed is recited in many fewer Protestant churches than it once was, and the categories set forth by the early councils are simply unknown to a majority of Christians. Some commentators may judge these categories well lost, but the point at issue here is simply that their disappearance opens the door to christological pluralism. The basic rubrics of Nicea and Chalcedon once played a major part in laying out the boundaries of christological orthodoxy. If those rubrics are now dismantled by theologians and are unknown to ordinary Christians, versions of Christ will appear on the scene that would have been impossible in the past.

A second important factor in the explosion of Christs within the churches is the privatization of religion, one of the hallmarks of the phenomenon of secularization in the modern and contemporary West. If religion, in the form of the Christian church, once had a powerful unifying role in Western society, that role was taken away by the forces of modernity. Those forces moved the economy into the center of Western society, relegating religion to a relatively apolitical role. Religion became largely a private matter, as opposed to a fully public one. This, in turn, paved the way for religious pluralism, for now each individual could choose his or her own religious route, as opposed to having that route dictated by a powerful religious institution holding sway over the spiritual inclinations of a whole society.[14] As a result, it seems quite natural to contemporary Christians that they should choose their own Christs of faith, however idiosyncratic those Christs might turn out to be. They are not forced to join a particular church, nor do they expect that the church that they do join will dictate to them exactly how they ought to believe. Faith in Christ is, after all, a personal matter. Furthermore, churches that have lost touch with the dictates of Nicea and Chalcedon may not have the theological tools with which to enforce christological uniformity, even if they chose to do so. Given these conditions, one should expect more and more Christs to appear.

A third important factor is the historical consciousness that has an effect on the majority of educated Christians now. Most contemporary Western Christians are well aware of the fact that there have been many different Christs down through Christian history, and that different social contexts produce different religious attitudes. Hence, they are conditioned to expect a diversity of Christs in our own day and age. Why should the person sitting next to me in church have exactly the same version of Christ that I do? That is simply not the way Christianity works, or so it seems to those schooled in the facts of Christian history and development. A pluralism of Christs seems a given for contemporary Christians, like gravity, or like the pluralism of the larger American society.

That larger social and cultural pluralism is the fourth factor that requires consideration. Our society is pluralistic through and through. It is made up of different ethnic groups, competing political and economic interests, diverse sets of moral values, conflicting tastes in both popular and high culture, and innumerable ways of being religious. This encompassing culture of pluralism affects those in the churches in at least two significant ways. First, it creates a mindset that expects pluralism and is used to operating with the freedom entailed by such pluralism. This mindset inevitably goes with Christians into their churches. Second, the actual content of this social pluralism is important: there are many religious options to choose from. Far from being limited to only one version of the Christ, I am free to choose some different religious guide alto-gether, such as the Buddha or the Koran. If I do in fact choose the Christ, the version of the Christ that I embrace will nonetheless have been influenced by my encounter with all of the other religious options arrayed before me. Christians today have a host of new resources for constructing Christs, and a large number of new Christs is almost surely going to result. As but one example, consider the fact that a significant number of followers of Christ now choose to approach him through forms of meditation modeled on Asian spiritual techniques. This choice as to *how* the believer unites with Christ necessarily affects *who* Christ is for the believer.

This fourth reason for internal christological pluralism—the impact upon the Christian tradition of the larger pluralistic society with all the religious resources it has to offer—illustrates the fact that we live in a world in which "practically all traditions have become porous," as David Tracy puts it in his major study of theological pluralism.[15] Com-mitment to a religious tradition, no matter how wholehearted, does not insulate one from the rest of one's society and the larger world. For a tradition to be healthy, it must have a permeable membrane, able to let in sources of nourishment from the external world while filtering out what is potentially harmful. In our own day, the pluralistic structure and mindset of our whole society assures tradition's openness. This openness must be kept in view if we are to understand the contemporary rela-tionship between the Christian tradition and its larger environment, and thus one of the mechanisms through which the tradition produces many Christs of faith.

It behooves us, then, to be wary of the kind of emphasis on tradi-tion currently in vogue among some Christian theologians of a more conservative sensibility. This emphasis would ignore the permeability of the membrane that bounds tradition in favor of a view of tradition as essentially self-sufficient. At the heart of this view is the desire to resist modernity. Much has been written about the ideological character of modernity, about how its particular notions of truth and reason and of the individual's relation to society have reinforced the power of some segments of Western society and disenfranchised others. The resistance of theologians to modernity tends to focus on two other issues, however. First, many theologians seek to reemphasize community, which they believe modernity undermined through its obsession with the individual and his or her rights. The second and more contentious issue is an epis-temological one. Theological resistance to modernity is often the result of a kind of Enlightenment-weariness, the desire to escape the burden of having to defend Christian belief before the court of modern reason. Modernity champions a universalist and foundationalist epistemology, according to which the only beliefs that we are justified in holding are those that have very particular characteristics: beliefs are justified when they are self-evident, or evident to the senses, or incorrigible, or when they follow from other beliefs that meet these impregnable, universal standards of rationality.[16]

This Enlightenment foundationalism, based as it is on a generally scientific approach to what constitutes evidence and justification, can create serious difficulties for religious belief. After all, religious convictions are usually about something that is, by its very nature, beyond the scope of ordinary ways to knowledge. Postmodern philosophers have suggested a variety of epistemological avenues on which we might leave behind this modern foundationalism, but the path of least resistance for many theologians is to argue that a religious tradition provides us with certain basic convictions that need not be defended, at least in the modern sense of rational defense. Two influential proponents of this approach to religious belief (and, by extension, to tradition) are Alvin Plantinga and George Lindbeck. While I cannot do justice here to the subtleties of their work, it is possible briefly to indicate the directions they take and to point to dangers in certain possible applications of their positions.[17]

Plantinga is the preeminent representative of what is known as Reformed epistemology, which is so named because it traces some of its motivating impulses to the Calvinist tradition. Reformed epistemologists and their modern foundationalist opponents agree that legitimate beliefs are of two sorts. Some of our beliefs are justified as conclusions from evidence, which evidence is derived from other beliefs that we hold. But, if we are to avoid an infinite regress, we cannot suppose that all of our beliefs rest on other beliefs. Our believing must simply begin somewhere: some of our beliefs must be basic beliefs, that is, beliefs not dependent upon other beliefs. It has usually been assumed that, if belief in God and other fundamental religious convictions are to be justified, they must follow as conclusions from other beliefs. But Plantinga suggests that such convictions can legitimately qualify as basic beliefs. Now Plantinga and his foundationalist opponents agree that we all operate with certain basic beliefs, those beliefs upon which our other beliefs rest. But they disagree about which sorts of beliefs are *properly* basic. Whereas the foundationalist holds that a basic belief must be self-evident, or evident to the senses, or incorrigible, Plantinga charges that this foundationalist claim is both internally incoherent and unable to account for the way in which we in fact form basic beliefs in daily life.[18] For Plantinga, I can quite properly count as a basic belief a simple memory belief such as, "I had breakfast this morning." This is a belief upon which I rightly base other beliefs, such as the belief that I will not need to eat again until noon. While the mere memory of having had breakfast this morning does not satisfy the foundationalist's criteria for basicality, it does provide grounds for my belief that I had breakfast.[19] Furthermore, the belief that I had breakfast because I remember doing so is just the kind of belief with which, in actual practice, we begin a chain of beliefs.

If this is how actual believing works, then the Christian need not, for example, come up with what the foundationalist would regard as evidence for the existence of God or the divinity of Christ. Rather, within the Christian community or tradition, belief in God and in the divinity of Christ are basic beliefs.[20] That is where Christians begin, and they have grounds in their particular experience of the world for doing so. Of course, other persons from other religious communities will not share these basic beliefs; they will begin somewhere else. What is more, there are no universal rational criteria that span different religious communities and allow us to adjudicate implicit arguments among communities. The Muslims' basic beliefs include the conviction that the Koran is the very word of Allah; Christians will disagree. Many Christians count among their basic beliefs that Christ died for our sins; Muslims hold no such belief. But there is no point in looking for some fundamental principles via which to prove that one community is right and the other wrong. Each community simply has its own basic beliefs, and those beliefs need make sense only for those within the community that embraces them.

George Lindbeck provides what I take to be a more sophisticated and nuanced version of anti-Enlightenment theory of religion. Yet it is possible to interpret his work in a way that leads to a Christian isolationism not entirely unlike Plantinga's. While Lindbeck is entirely open to the possibility of dialogue among subtraditions of Christianity—his most important work has been in the service of the ecumenical dialogue—he doubts that different traditions such as Christianity and Buddhism have much to say to one another. His "cultural-linguistic" approach to theology suggests that all religious beliefs and the experiences that accompany them are rooted in certain linguistic frameworks. Just as Wittgenstein's forms of life are correlated with language games that have their own internal principles of usage and meaningfulness, the religious claims made by Christians are set forth in a particular set of language games correlated with the Christian form of life. Christian assertions find their meaning in the context of these language games alone, not in terms of other games. As in Plantinga's position, there is no common framework here in which it is possible to adjudicate apparently competing religious claims. Indeed, some religions perhaps just cannot communicate with one another at all. Lindbeck tells us that "when affirmations or ideas from categorially different religious or philosophical frameworks are introduced into a given religious outlook, these are either simply babbling or else, like mathematical formulas employed in a poetic text, they have vastly different functions and meanings than they had in their original settings."[21] Thus, each religion becomes a separate cultural-linguistic world unto itself. Far from having to defend itself before some Enlightenment tribunal of universal reason, the very notion of such a defense is hopelessly confused.

Plantinga is one of this era's most influential philosophers of religion; Lindbeck has spent a professional lifetime sensitively attuned to the possibilities of dialogue among Christian subtraditions, especially between Roman Catholicism and his own Lutheranism. Thus, neither of these thinkers can fairly be accused of a wholly insular theological position. But at least according to some possible readings of their respective positions, it seems that Enlightenment-weariness has resulted in a hermetic view of tradition. From that vantage point, my religious community is responsible only to itself for what it believes, not to the larger society or human community. My community has one set of basic beliefs, your community has another, and never the twain shall meet; I am ensconced in my cultural-linguistic religious framework so that I cannot make sense of your religious beliefs and experiences, nor you of mine. And the most significant pay-off in all of this is that neither of us needs to argue for or defend our beliefs outside of our respective self-contained communities or traditions.

One can locate this theological position historically by noting that, in essence, it is what results when the "God of the gaps" meets postmodernism. The theological strategy associated with the God of the gaps was to say that, even though modern science is continually explaining things in purely mundane terms that used to be explained by reference to God, we can point to the gaps that remain in our scientific knowledge of the universe as the place where God is to be found. In other words, this strategy sought to find a sanctuary for belief in God, a safe-haven where that belief could not be challenged by the intellectual programs of modernity, modern science in particular. The approach taken by the Reformed epistemologists, as well as by many of those such as Lindbeck who draw upon Wittgenstein to support their theological agenda, is also to put theistic belief in a place safely beyond the range of external intellectual challenge. But in this instance safety is provided not by the gaps in the content of our knowledge, but by the unbridgeable gaps that postmodern antifoundationalism sees between the different traditions or cultural-linguistic frameworks that generate that knowledge.

Of course, merely to understand the historical location and motivation of this program is not to demonstrate its falsehood or inadequacy. Numerous commentators have, however, attempted to point out what

they regard as the philosophical difficulties in the positions advanced by
Plantinga and Lindbeck.[22] But the main issue, for our purposes, is less
philosophical than practical: simply stated, the notion of religious traditions or communities as self-contained worlds is just *empirically* false.
Traditions are much more permeable than Plantinga and Lindbeck let
on. Contemporary Christians not only can communicate with both
other subtraditions and other religions, they are doing so continuously.
Christians today actually borrow insights and practices from those other
religious traditions in their creation of Christs of faith. Consider another
concrete example: it is now quite possible for a Christian to augment his
or her concept of sin, which in the past might have been understood
almost exclusively in terms of rebellion against God, with the Buddhist
notion of attachment. Of course, the Buddhist insights are modified
when they are fused with Christian sensibilities about the self. The
Christian is unlikely to perceive the self as ultimately an illusion. But this
hardly suggests that insights and practices borrowed from elsewhere
take on a wholly different meaning in their new context, as if their
meaning within Christian faith were simply discontinuous with their use
in the traditions of their origin. If they were thoroughly discontinuous,
the Christian would be unable to make anything of them in the first
place; there would be nothing to borrow and nothing to adapt. The Buddhist insights and practices are attractive to the Christian precisely
because they connect with convictions and needs within his or her own
Christianity.[23] But Plantinga and Lindbeck, in their understandable urge
to throw off the burden of continually defending Christian belief in the
kind of universal conversation proposed by the Enlightenment, have
crafted an account of religious community and tradition as self-contained and of insights from different traditions as incommensurable. As
a result, their picture of tradition ends up as wistful prescription, rather
than as a description of what is in fact the case.

The fundamental temptation at issue here is that of avoiding the
need to defend one's religious beliefs outside the comfortable confines of
one's own tradition, and specific characteristics of the Christian tradition itself may heighten that temptation. Plantinga and Lindbeck are
Protestants. As a result of their Protestant heritage, one would not
expect them to gravitate as quickly to the notion of tradition as some of
their Catholic compatriots. But their focus on a particular religious community's set of basic beliefs, or on the cultural-linguistic framework that
defines religious sensibilities, dovetails with the notion of tradition. The
element of Protestantism that might most readily encourage their epis-
temological retreat to a self-enclosed tradition is the principle of *sola
fide*, faith alone, which sometimes finds expression in fideism.[24] That is,
some Protestant thinkers have been tempted to abandon the responsi-

bility to provide reasons for their faith and have opted for a blind "leap of faith."[25] The most potent form of this Protestant fideism in the present day is provided by the theology of Karl Barth, and the sensibilities of thinkers such as Plantinga and Lindbeck might initially be regarded as neo-Barthian. But Barth would issue as powerful a "No!" to their theologies as he did to Emil Brunner's flirtation with natural theology. For Barth, human reason is impotent to know God because of God's thoroughgoing transcendence of the finite sphere. We come to knowledge of God, if at all, only through God's gracious revelation of himself, wherein he deigns to be immanent as well as transcendent. Thus, there is neither any need nor any possibility of defending Christian belief in terms of some culturally regnant school of philosophy.

Plantinga and Lindbeck also hold that Christian belief cannot and need not be so defended. But their reason for this contention is not the infinite distance between God and human noetic capacities that is at issue for Barth, but rather certain features of all human belief. My inability, and lack of need, to defend belief in God is formally similar for Plantinga to the fact that it is unnecessary for me to defend argumentatively the basic belief that I had breakfast this morning. For Lindbeck it is formally similar to the way in which many beliefs in a cultural-linguistic framework cannot meaningfully be transferred into other frameworks. In other words, while Barth holds that Christian belief is beyond any attempt at universally understandable rational defense because of the majesty of God, Plantinga and Lindbeck put Christian belief beyond any such defense by making it formally comparable to totally mundane beliefs and practices.

Due to the Protestant predilection for fideism, thinkers such as Plantinga and Lindbeck may be all the more encouraged to adopt, in however un-Barthian a fashion, a view of tradition as self-enclosed. But what of their Catholic brothers and sisters? Catholic thinkers, of course, have historically been more interested in the notion of tradition than have Protestants. One might expect, however, that Catholic theologians would also be more hesitant about ghettoizing the notion of tradition, given Catholicism's commitment to natural theology. The concept of natural theology entails that, far from it being impossible to communicate about religious beliefs outside the tradition of their origin, the structure of the world and the universal structures of human reason make it possible for all intelligent persons to come to agreement on such fundamental issues as the existence of God. This perspective finds its classic expression in the theology of Thomas Aquinas, and is articulated as official church teaching by the First Vatican Council.[26]

On the other hand, practice does not always follow theory. Thus, if the Roman Catholic Church appears to be threatened by forces in the surrounding culture, some Catholics will be tempted to retreat to the Catholic tradition as if it could be closed up like Noah's ark: one can then ride out the storm while the rest of humanity goes under. And there are at least some in Catholic circles who, like the Protestant antifoundationalists, find modernity repugnant and wish to overturn the Enlightenment emphasis on universal standards of belief and practice. One of the loudest Catholic protesters against modernity in recent years has been the moral philosopher Alisdair MacIntyre.[27] It is precisely to the concept of tradition that MacIntyre turns as an antidote to modern universalism. MacIntyre's attack upon modern Western liberalism is a no-holds-barred frontal assault, yet his concept of tradition is a nuanced one. He is most interested in traditions of inquiry, which he defines as "an argument extended through time in which certain fundamental agreements are defined and redefined in terms of two kinds of conflict: those with critics and enemies external to the tradition . . . and those internal, interpretive debates through which the meaning and rationale of the fundamental agreements come to be expressed and by whose progress a tradition is constituted."[28] Thus, while MacIntyre is adamant about contrasting the self-contained character of tradition with what he regards as an illusory modern universalism, he allows that there are ways for different traditions to test one another.[29]

MacIntyre has tended to focus his attentions upon very specific ethical and theological traditions, most notably, Aristotelianism, Augustinianism, and Thomism. But can the Roman Catholic tradition taken as a whole be regarded as a self-contained tradition, a concrete contradiction of Enlightenment pretensions to universal standards of value and meaning? What requires much more analysis here is how such a position squares with Catholicism's own interpretation of itself as a tradition. Catholic thinkers have never understood their tradition as one tradition among others, a tradition displaying the general characteristics of human tradition. Rather, they have from the beginning seen the core of the Catholic tradition as *divine* tradition.[30] Yves Congar reminds us, for example, that Paul already condemned "human tradition" (in Colossians 2:8).[31] One need not believe that there is such a thing as divine tradition in order to grasp the point here: if we are to be true to the self-understanding of Catholic tradition, we cannot attribute to it the anti-universalism that MacIntyre and others imply belongs to the general category of tradition. On the contrary, the Roman Catholic notion of tradition is peculiarly open-ended: tradition as the passing on of the revelation of God contains a message intended for and graspable by all humankind, however much it might be couched in a vocabulary that initially appears parochial. To bound this tradition in such a way that it loses its universal purview is to "humanize" it in the pejorative sense of the term, that is, to turn it in upon itself in a way that the Catholic tradition itself could only see as a function of human fallenness.

Of course, any religious tradition might claim that it is universal in the sense that it provides those within the tradition a guide for understanding the whole of reality. But the universality connected with the Catholic tradition's sense of divine revelation must include a universality of access. If God had revealed himself within a tradition that was simply incommensurable with the worldviews of persons outside it, then the vast majority of those outsiders would, in effect, be predestined never to have the benefit of divine revelation. But such predestinationist sensibilities are foreign to the Catholic tradition, which explicitly rejected the element of predestination in Augustine's thought, for example, despite the great respect it has otherwise accorded that eminent father of the church. If divine revelation is vouchsafed the tradition of the church, that tradition must make immediate contact with the worldviews of persons outside it, so that they can readily grasp the value of entering the Christian tradition.[32] This commitment to the possibility of universal communication is apparent when the bishops at the Second Vatican Council declare that "in the light of Christ . . . the Council wishes to speak to all men."[33] And it is constantly in evidence in John Paul II's encyclical, *Fides et Ratio*, in which there are over twenty-five references to universality.[34]

Where does our overview of Christian tradition and christological pluralism leave us, then? In order to be able to say that when I use the word "Christ," I am referring to essentially the same reality intended by that word in the past, my christological constructions must be rooted in the Christian tradition. To put the same thing in slightly different terms, rooting my talk of Christ in the Christian tradition provides my Christ or Christs with a degree of objectivity; it protects christologies from the charge of being mere subjective projections. This connection with the Christian tradition hardly quashes christological pluralism, however. On the contrary, christological pluralism has been a part of the Christian tradition throughout its history. And in our own day, when a more general pluralistic dynamic powers the societies in which the Christian tradition must live, that tradition is necessarily a permeable membrane. It remains for us to see whether it is possible to find some meaningful pattern in the midst of this christological pluralism.

CHAPTER 3

Christ-Testing

In the previous chapter, we indicated the Christian tradition's role in providing the context within which genuine Christs can appear, and we considered the general relationship of the Christian tradition and its subtraditions to christological pluralism. Now we are faced with the task of coming up with specific criteria for deciding which Christs of faith can be genuine. Because this is potentially a very presumptuous undertaking, we need to think carefully about how to proceed, rather than jumping right into the task of articulating criteria. What are the options here?

If one identifies with an individual subtradition of the Christian faith, one possibility would be to turn to the specific dictates of particular confessions of faith that have informed that subtradition. Thus, one might look to the Augsburg Confession, or the Heidelberg Catechism, or the contemporary Catechism of the Catholic Church, and apply its dictates to various Christs of faith to see if those Christs measure up. But, given what we have discovered about the nature of tradition in the contemporary West, there is a problem with any procedure that would too quickly retreat to highly specific and parochial christological guidelines. The problem exists, at least, for those who conceive of faith-guidelines as growing in a natural fashion out of the convictions and experiences of the persons who make up a tradition, rather than being imposed artificially. For we have seen that the contemporary subtraditions of the Christian faith, and hence the Christian tradition taken as a whole, are bounded by highly permeable membranes. Subtraditions today are characterized by an extraordinary degree of internal pluralism. If we are to be true to the nature of tradition itself, then we have to be careful not to reach for criteria that too quickly quash christological pluralism.

But even if we do remain sensitive to the internally pluralistic nature of contemporary tradition, we are still faced with the challenge of striking some kind of balance between christological pluralism and the factors guaranteeing a tradition's integrity. It is to be hoped, of course, that a tradition's identity and the pluralism within it are not mutually exclusive. But even if identity and pluralism are ultimately complementary, it is inevitable that some interpreters will lean more toward the protection of identity in their attempt to effect the proper balance, while others will lean toward pluralism. It will come as no surprise, given my focus on christological pluralism thus far, that I shall opt for the latter interpretive stance.

Another issue to be considered, before specifying actual criteria, is the manner in which the criteria will be applied. It is tempting to suppose that one could set forth specific christological criteria and then quickly and unproblematically determine whether a particular Christ of faith possessed the characteristics specified in the criteria. In practice, of course, any procedure for Christ-testing will prove more ambiguous. First of all, as we noted in the preceding chapter, any principles of christological orthodoxy by which we might choose to judge new Christs will themselves be in a constant process of development. Thanks to the manner in which the subtraditions act back upon the larger tradition, as well as to the tradition's interaction with the social and cultural settings in which it finds itself, the Christian tradition provides no rigid christological principles, but only floating criteria. Furthermore, even when we have settled on certain criteria, we shall still be faced with the difficult interpretive task of deciding whether a Christ does or does not meet the criteria. Here too, ambiguity can easily enter the equation. The situation is analogous to literary criticism: two critics who operate with similar aesthetic criteria may still disagree about the merits of a particular novel. In short, there is no way to line up a Christ of faith alongside a set of criteria and simply check off in mechanical fashion which criteria that particular Christ of faith meets. But this way of applying criteria is not the mode of Christ-testing that we shall explore in any case. Rather than demanding that Christs clearly *display* characteristics specified in the criteria, we shall ask that Christs of faith seriously *address* the issues represented by the criteria. This procedure allows for the kind of change and development that has characterized the Christian tradition from the beginning, and that may necessarily accelerate in our pluralistic age.

Consider a concrete example. Suppose that someone advances the criterion that Christs of faith must provide redemption from sin. Some Christs of faith may straightforwardly exhibit this motif. Others may de-emphasize it. But the issue for Christs that have little apparent connection with redemption from sin, then, will be whether persons who champion these Christs of faith at least take the venerable notion of redemption from sin sufficiently seriously that they go to the trouble of showing why that notion should now be regarded as less important. Some feminist theologians have argued, for instance, that the traditional emphasis on sin and redemption is destructive for women, in that it only reinforces the tendencies to self-denigration inculcated in them by a sexist society. According to these thinkers, the traditional concepts of sin and redemption must be modified substantially; the notion of redemption should be replaced by or conceived in terms of liberation, including liberation from the results of oppressive forces such as sexism.[1] Some might conclude, given how we are suggesting that christological criteria be applied, that these thinkers have effectively grappled with the criterion via their arguments about why it should be abandoned or radically changed. Their Christs of faith would pass the proposed test, then, by seriously addressing the criterion at issue. And this particular way of addressing the criterion is an example of how a tradition develops and how criteria can change over time.

At the same time, to proceed by asking whether Christs of faith address particular criteria, rather than whether they display characteristics specified in the criteria, is not to escape the need for interpretation and the possibility of controversy. Who is to decide, for example, whether a particular feminist version of Christ that has abandoned the notion of redemption from personal sin has successfully addressed the criterion—different interpreters might well decide the issue differently— and what principles will the interpreter employ in making that judgment? Does the interpreter need carefully articulated criteria for determining when the criterion that Christ must provide redemption has been successfully addressed, that is, criteria for applying criteria? Unless one is willing to pursue a potentially infinite regress here, he or she must once again be reconciled to the risk entailed in any act of interpretation.

The question of who will apply the criteria is connected with the decision as to which particular criteria will be employed. Does each individual interpreter specify his or her own criteria? As for the present investigation, my intention is not to pick criteria that I alone wish to apply to various Christs in an idiosyncratic act of christological winnowing, but to suggest criteria that have been at work for a long time in the history of competition among Christs of faith.

The decision about which particular criteria to employ entails another balancing act. On the one hand, the criteria should be sufficiently specific that they can perform some actual work. They must serve the attempt to discern which Christs of faith have a significant link with what persons have meant by Christ in the past, so that we can determine which present-day Christs are genuine. The criteria must make it possible, in the end, to reject some Christs of faith. On the other hand, the criteria must be broad enough to respect the reality of christological pluralism. Criteria that would rule out the majority of Christs right from the beginning simply will not do justice to the creativity of the contemporary christological scene. Keeping in view this need to balance the criteria's flexibility with their capacity to do some real sorting, along with the desire to specify criteria actually at work in the history of the conversation within the Christian tradition, I propose three basic and familiar criteria in the search for genuine Christs of faith. First, genuine Christs of faith should bear a clear family resemblance to the Christs found in the New Testament. Second, genuine Christs of faith must reflect the traditional confession that Christ is God. Third, genuine Christs need to do justice to the claim that Christ provides redemption. Because these three criteria, at least on the surface, represent old and familiar mainstream christological principles, there would be little point in simply repeating them here. The point is not to rehash them, but to explore their relation to the pluralistic challenge that is at the center of our concerns. That relation is at least twofold. First, of course, we need to consider how the criteria might allow us to sort through a multitude of Christs. Second, it is important to explore the pluralism that characterizes the criteria themselves, that is, the constant development and diverse articulations that are part of the history of the criteria.

FAMILY RESEMBLANCE TO NEW TESTAMENT CHRISTS

That a genuine Christ will be recognizably related to the Christs of the New Testament seems a given. Almost everyone who has ever presented an interpretation of Christ and wanted that Christ to be in harmony with the larger history of the Christian tradition has claimed biblical warrant for the interpretation. The New Testament has ever been the most important touchstone of christological orthodoxy. But rather than simply taking this as a brute fact about the Christian tradition, we can briefly consider some of the reasons for continuing to expect harmony with the New Testament from our Christs.

First of all, and most simply, the New Testament is the single largest source of information available on the life and teaching of Jesus and his reception as the Christ. Furthermore, that reception is a relatively early one. In other words, while the New Testament already presents us with Christs of faith rather than the Jesus of history, it represents a period of Christ-creation that is only a step or two removed from the disciples' original response to the actual man Jesus. Thus, we might say that, while the New Testament gives us no direct access to Jesus of Nazareth as a historical figure, it keeps us in proximity to the historical Jesus, which is one essential pole of the total event of Jesus as the Christ. And without constant reference to the New Testament accounts of early responses to Jesus as the Christ, it would be all-too-easy to lose touch with the historical pole. Each generation produces new imaginary Christs of faith, usually informed in large part by the Christs produced in the previous generation. But this means that there are innumerable stages between the very first reception of the man Jesus as the Christ and today's Christs of faith. What prevents this ongoing process of Christ-production from mirroring the old game of "telephone"? If my contemporary imaginary Christ is a response to an earlier generation of Christs of faith, and they in turn responded to the generation preceding them, and so on for centuries, is it not quite possible that my Christ no longer bears any traces of Jesus of Nazareth? The process of Christ-formation is best protected from this danger by responding not only to the imaginary Christs of the preceding generation, but by seeing to it that one's Christ of faith is always a response too to the Christs of the New Testament.

Second, we have already noted that, in order to bring objectivity to our Christs of faith so that these Christs in some sense refer to the same reality intended by persons in the past when they spoke of Christ, we must orient Christs of faith by the Christian tradition. And the Christian tradition has, of course, perennially tested its Christs for their conformity to the New Testament. Noncanonical gospels can supplement our grasp of Christs of faith, perhaps even suggesting hitherto underexplored avenues for christological development, but precisely because they never achieved canonical status, they cannot serve as well as the New Testament as touchstones of objectivity. In other words, conformity to the Christs found in the noncanonical gospels cannot as effectively insure that the Christ of which I speak is, in the end, the same reality intended by persons who spoke of Christ in the past.[2]

The need for some kind of objectivity in the production of Christs of faith, so that my Christ of faith does not end up being a wholly arbitrary projection of my own subjectivity, suggests a third reason for holding to the New Testament pictures of Christ as a criterion: the New Testament is a text or collection of texts, and thus possesses its own particular kind of otherness and objectivity. A text is a reality existing independently of me. I am not the source of its meaning. Thus, if I do attempt to take the text's independence seriously, the text might serve to limit, and perhaps even overturn, some of my assumptions.

Fourth, there is an important sense in which New Testament Christs have passed the test of practical efficacy. In other words, the versions of Christ presented in the New Testament are Christs that members of the early Christian community found to be effective bearers of what they sought in their quest for salvation. It is for this reason, one might argue, and not only due to considerations of apostolic origin, that these particular Christs found their way into the New Testament. What is more, these New Testament Christs have continued to prove their efficacy down through the ages as generation after generation of Christians has put them into practice. This is what thinkers such as Tillich have in mind when they argue that we do not need to worry about whether the New Testament gives us an accurate sense of the historical Jesus, since the biblical picture of Jesus as the Christ—we might better say the biblical pictures—provides a kind of existential self-validation by communicating the "New Being" to those who embrace that biblical picture.[3] While the practical requirements of the religious quest may vary with time and circumstance, so that it is reasonable to entertain the possibility that the Christs set forth in the New Testament might someday lose their practical salvific efficacy, we should at least start with the assumption that the New Testament provides us with Christs that have proved their worth in the concrete struggle to attain a religiously significant life.

Lest these four considerations suggest that the New Testament provides a wholly unerring basis for Christ-testing, that impression must be balanced by a recognition of the overwhelming pluralism of New Testament interpretation over the centuries. Just in our own era, and confining ourselves to the matter of worship, the New Testament portraits of Christ are used to warrant everything from Appalachian snake handling to Mass at Saint Peter's Basilica. Contemporary hermeneutical theory, with its rejection of the hermeneutics of authorial intent, for example, suggests that there can be numerous genuinely legitimate interpretations of a text. But the history of New Testament interpretation and "use" surely goes beyond a wholly unproblematic pluralism. While the New Testament texts must, as texts, have a particular kind of otherness and objectivity, Christian history demonstrates the possibility of riding roughshod over that otherness. It is apparently a tempting and easy affair to use the New Testament as a screen upon which to project one's own, or a community's, wishes and prejudices. And New Testament scholarship has taught us that the gospels themselves are already the result, in part, of early Christian communities projecting their assumptions and prejudices upon the figure of Jesus. All interpretation involves risk, and New Testament interpretation would appear to involve more than its share. Hence, the criterion of family resemblance with the portraits of Christ found in the New Testament does not provide a surefire method of Christ-testing, but only a starting point.

CHRIST IS GOD

The claim that Christ is the very presence of God has been a defining component of the Christian tradition. Yet, for all its centrality, the claim has been unpacked in extraordinarily diverse ways. The history of the claim is a powerful example of the constant interpretive movement characterizing Christian belief. As we noted earlier, the New Testament contains numerous titles for and claims about Christ. Some of them, such as the title "Son of God" or the Johannine "The Father and I are one" (John 10:30), clearly suggest a special relationship between Christ and God, but they do so without indicating in any precise or technical way just how that relationship should be conceptualized. Much the same can be said about the articles of the Apostle's Creed, the "oldest Roman catechism":

> I believe in God, the Father almighty, creator of heaven and earth.
> I believe in Jesus Christ, his only Son, our Lord.
> He was conceived by the power of the Holy Spirit and born of the Virgin Mary.
> He suffered under Pontius Pilate, was crucified, died, and was buried.
> He descended into hell. On the third day he rose again.
> He ascended into heaven and is seated at the right hand of the Father.
> He will come again to judge the living and the dead.
> I believe in the Holy Spirit, the holy catholic Church, the communion of the saints, the forgiveness of sins, the resurrection of the body, and the life everlasting. Amen.[4]

To say that Christ is the Son of God, that he rose from the dead, and that he will return at the end of time to judge all human beings, is certainly to give him an extraordinary status and to see him as uniquely related to God. But the Apostle's Creed does not spell out for us the precise nature of that unique relationship. The assertions of the Creed could, for instance, be judged consistent with the claim that Jesus Christ is a supernatural being created by God, or even a man imbued by God with special powers.

It is with the Council of Nicea, of course, in the year 325, that we encounter the most influential attempt to specify just how Christ is the presence of God: he is, say the Nicene fathers, of the very same substance, *homoousios*, with the Father. Thus, when the Nicene Creed is formulated, reflecting as it does the contentious deliberations surrounding the Council of Nicea, as well as the work of the Council of Constantinople in 381, we are presented with an apparently unambiguous avowal that Christ manifests the presence of God inasmuch as he actually *is* God:

> We believe in one Lord, Jesus Christ, the only Son of God eternally begotten of the Father, God from God, Light from Light, true God from true God, begotten, not made, one in Being with the Father. Through him all things were made.[5]

If Nicea provides a rule for talking about the relationship of Christ to God the Father, the Council of Chalcedon in 451 attempts to outline the relationship of Christ's humanity to his divinity: Jesus Christ is one unified person with two natures, fully God and fully man.

But however significant such conciliar formulas, they seldom proved a straightjacket for Christian piety, despite what modern critics would sometimes have us believe. We need to recall again at this point that the *homoousios* formula, for example, has not been understood by its best interpreters as a positive explanation that pins down the exact character of the divinity of Christ. Rather than filling in the blanks in our knowledge of the divine nature and its place in the being of Jesus Christ, Nicea simply provided some formal boundaries for thinking and talking about Christ. As Bernard Lonergan puts it, commenting upon Athanasius' interpretation of Nicea as a rule for our thinking, "What the rule states is that what is said of the Father is also to be said of the Son, except that the Son is Son and not Father."[6] That Christ is God is clear from this rule; what it means for him to be God and how exactly we should express the divinity of the Father and the Son is left to the imagination of post-Nicene Christians down through ages.

If we are to evaluate the belief that Christ is God, we must begin by reminding ourselves that Christians will say that they make the assertion that Christ is God because that assertion is true. In other words, the fundamental significance of the assertion is not a function of our needs and wishes but, rather, of what is the case about reality. But this does not change the fact, first of all, that Christians initially arrived at the conclusion that Christ is God as the result of practical considerations. They considered what had to be true about Christ for Christ to be able to provide salvation. Furthermore, even if something is true independently of how we react to it, it is inevitable that we shall evaluate its implications for our own concrete existence. Thus, what are we to make, in practical terms, of the notion that Christ is God?

Let us begin with some possible negative interpretations of what might motivate someone to hold that Christ is God in the flesh. As I have just indicated, early Christian thinkers were concerned with the divinity of Christ as a prerequisite for his ability to provide salvation.[7] But while it may be true that only God can offer salvation, could not God do so by acting through something that is less than God? Why does Christ actually have to *be* God? Is there an anxious grasping for security behind the traditional Christian claim that Christ is God? Perhaps Christians have made the strong and even paradoxical claim that Christ is God out of a desire to be absolutely certain that, via faith in Christ, they have a hold upon salvation. And this sort of unrealistic desire, so it

might be argued, bespeaks an unhealthy inability to live with any degree
of uncertainty or contingency.

As a closely related charge, consider the possibility that Christian
avowals of the divinity of Christ are tantamount to a flight from finitude. The harsh challenges of finite existence are perhaps too much for
Christians to bear, so they seek an escape from the finite by looking to
a spiritual teacher whom they aver is not merely a finite human being,
but God himself in the flesh. Of course, it is precisely the "in the flesh"
part of the traditional Christian claims about Christ that distinguishes
orthodox Christianity from its gnostic varieties, which often manifest a
disdain for the finite world. Still, even mainline christological belief has
been constantly tempted by docetism, the heresy according to which
Christ merely appears to be human.

A third negative possibility is that belief in Christ as God is driven
by a passionate desire for exclusivity: "There are many religious teach-
ers and even a fair number of genuine prophets, but the figure whom *we*
follow is actually God." Thus, no other religious guide can begin to
compete with Jesus Christ. In the words of the Jesus set forth in the
Gospel of John, "I am the way, and the truth, and the life. No one comes
to the Father except through me." (John 14:6). Such exclusivist claims
are clearly tied up with issues of power, inasmuch as the claim to be in
touch with the one and only divine guide can be used to impose the will
of one's own group upon others.[8]

But certainly the Christian desire to fully identify Jesus Christ with
God can also be put more positively. For one thing, as the theology of
Karl Barth suggests, there may be a natural trajectory leading from the
claim that Christ is a revelation of God to the claim that Christ in fact
is God. If Christ is to genuinely reveal God, then he cannot present God
in a way that is somehow true for us in our relation to God, but not
really true of God in himself. And if what Christ reveals is the very being
of God himself, then, so the argument goes, Christ must be God. Thus,
for a theologian such as Barth, it is not simply the particular content of
Christian revelation that points to the doctrine of the Trinity. Rather,
the bare fact that Christ and the Holy Spirit genuinely reveal God points
to the idea that they, along with the Father, are God.

A second consideration on the positive side of the ledger is to note
how belief in the divinity of Christ can be tied, not to the desire to escape
finitude, but to the most exalted aspirations regarding what human
beings can become. The Eastern fathers frequently cite the dictum that
Christ became man so that we might become divine. With their doctrine
of *theosis*, they present the idea that salvation entails not just forgiveness
of sin and righteous behavior, but actual participation in the being of
God.[9] That the desire for participation in God represented by the claim

that Jesus is God need not involve any suggestion of escape from our actual human condition is demonstrated by Karl Rahner's theological anthropology. Rahner allows us to read human being as including, as a gracious but constituent element, the presence of God to human consciousness. This consciousness of God begins as something unthematic, a presupposition of our awareness of the world rather than a discrete object of awareness. It provides the infinite horizon within which all of our acts of knowing and acting take place. The character of our existence is defined by how we respond to this constant presence of God, a presence brought to perfect thematization and clarity in the revelation of God in Jesus Christ. If the constant presence of God to human consciousness is a constitutive component of our being, then to open ourselves fully to this presence and seek participation in the being of God is not to escape from finitude, but to achieve the end for which human being has been created. Indeed, in terms of this theological anthropology, the claim that Christ is the God-man, while always finally a mystery for human understanding, need not appear as a category mistake. For now Christ's divinity can be understood as the perfect fulfillment of his humanity.[10]

However one evaluates Christianity's claim that Christ is God—whether as anxious, escapist and exclusive, or as appropriate and life-affirming—the fact remains that it has been definitive of the Christian faith. When modern and contemporary Christian thinkers turn to this claim, they often begin by issuing the familiar complaints about the substantialist metaphysic they believe is behind the definitions of Nicea and Chalcedon. Yet, they are invariably able to affirm that Christ is the presence of God. They simply do so in a way that is not dependent upon the particular philosophical worldview and vocabulary that they believe is enshrined in the ancient ecumenical councils. Thus we find Schleiermacher, the nineteenth-century initiator of modern theology, rejecting the literal implications of the conciliar definitions at the same time that he can affirm that Christ's perfect awareness of his absolute dependence upon God was "a veritable existence of God in him."[11] And at the end of the twentieth century, Jürgen Moltmann opens his systematic christology by explaining, "I am trying to think of Christ no longer statically, as one person in two natures. . . . I am trying to grasp him dynamically, in the forward movement of God's history with the world."[12] To hold to the claim that Christ is God, then, does not necessarily mean echoing literally the Nicene *homoousios* doctrine or the Chalcedonian principle of one person and two natures. Rather it means honoring the spirit of Nicea and Chalcedon by averring that Christ is in some fashion the very presence of God. Even in this less exacting form, however, the claim is still a strong one. For it suggests that Christ does not simply tell us about God, but actually provides access to God.

It is appropriate to recall Mircea Eliade's notion of the *axis mundi* in this context.[13] Eliade maintains that one encounters throughout the history of religions the figure of the pole at the center of the world, the symbolism of a vertical connection between this world and the world above. The *axis mundi* is, in other words, an accessway to the transcendent. The cross of Christ easily can be seen as one figure of the *axis mundi*, in that Christians have embraced it as the indispensable means of access to God. Christ is God in the sense of being the very presence of God, and that means, in turn, that Christ provides access to God.

The task of expressing in contemporary terms how Christ might be considered the presence of God involves more than just grappling with the admittedly thorny issue of how God can appear within the confines of space and time. There is a prior matter to be considered, namely, how one is to conceive of God at all. We cannot very well explain how Christ can make God present if we are unclear as to what we mean by God, or if we have not dealt with the pressure exerted upon traditional concepts of God by the forces of modernity and postmodernity. The essays contributed by a group of British theologians to the volume entitled *The Myth of God Incarnate* bring this fact home.[14] Each contributor reiterates the present inadequacy of the traditional doctrine of the incarnation of God in Christ with its dependence on the Nicene and Chalcedonian categories. At the same time, most of the authors still want to hold that Christ is the presence of God in some sense. They are concerned with "how it is that we, like our predecessors, have met God disclosed in the man, Jesus."[15] They tend to want to reaffirm the Pauline claim that "God was in Christ reconciling the world to himself."[16] Yet these writers have next to nothing to say about how we are to conceive and affirm God in the contemporary era. Dennis Nineham does point out, in the epilogue, that today we need a new imaginative picture of the relation of God to the world.[17] But neither he nor any of the other contributors to *The Myth of God Incarnate* bothers to ponder what such a picture might be. As a result, the book fails to advance significantly the discussion of contemporary christology.

The lesson here is that, if we are to use the notion of Christ as God as a criterion, we need to pay careful attention to what is meant by God in different versions of that notion. How shall we conceive the reality of God? Any survey of how the word "God" has been employed in the history of Western religion, or even just within Christianity, would confront us with yet another bracing dose of pluralism. The most familiar notion of God to be found within the Christian tradition, especially on the popular level, sees God as a supernatural personal consciousness who created the world, sustains it, and intervenes in its causal processes from time to time as he sees fit. This venerable perspective tends to think of God as a being who is essentially independent of the rest of reality: God has created the universe and it is dependent upon him, but he is not dependent upon the universe. It is customary to contrast this view of God with the panentheistic model, in which the universe is somehow a part of God's being; it exists "within" God. We find variations on this panentheistic model in the theologies of Friedrich Schleiermacher, Karl Rahner, and Paul Tillich, as well as in the "process" theology derived from the philosophy of Alfred North Whitehead.[18] Some varieties of Christian panentheism, such as that advanced by Rahner, continue to maintain that God is, in some recognizable sense of the terms, a personal consciousness who wills and acts. Other varieties, such as the version set forth by Tillich, tend to suggest that God is transpersonal—that deity is the ground of human personal consciousness but cannot itself be a personal consciousness. There are also influential theologies today that, pertinent to our emphasis on the role of imagination in grasping the transcendent, highlight the imaginative character of our concepts of God and counsel great reserve about the extent to which those concepts can be said to mirror the reality of God in Godself. One thinks here of the theologies of Gordon Kaufman and Sallie McFague, for example.[19] Yet another perspective on God, one even more radically nonmetaphysical than the perspectives offered by Kaufman and McFague, is provided by those thinkers who, prodded by various intellectual and pragmatic exigencies of the contemporary world, suggest that God in Godself is somehow a function of human belief and action. It is easy to find critiques of Christian theism that take this approach, of course, as in the work of Ludwig Feuerbach and of Sigmund Freud.[20] But there are also modern and contemporary thinkers who attempt to advance versions of this view that preserve some sense of genuine divine transcendence and that can function in the context of religious faith and commitment. John Dewey moved in this direction in the first half of the twentieth century.[21] A more recent variety of this general approach is provided by prominent feminist theologians such as Carol Christ and Rosemary Radford Ruether, at least according to one interpretation of their work. Their descriptions of deity can be read as implying that God or Goddess is not an independent being, but a function of individuals relating to other persons, nature, and the "power of being" in a particular attitude of self-transcendence. To enact this relation is to become conscious of one's rootedness in the larger universe round about us and of one's responsibilities and opportunities vis-à-vis the other beings and forces that make it up. This expansive relation works back on persons who enact it, and can be experienced as gracious and transformative.[22] It is a version of the divine that combines genuine transcendence with the powerful immanence demanded by many feminist thinkers, as well as by other religious thinkers concerned with issues such as the ecological crisis.

One could easily add other models to this brief sketch of contemporary options for envisioning God. But whichever model of God is operative in a particular christology, the claim ought to be that Jesus as the Christ makes that God present; Christ is the very presence of God in the sense of providing his followers access to God. Yet there is a danger in the assumption that, whatever new models of God come down the pike, Christians should simply press Jesus Christ into service as the manifestation of such deities. Edward Schillebeeckx imagines a possible scenario, for example, in which contemporary persons have what are in fact wholly new experiences of God, but they associate them with the experience of God mediated by Jesus:

> because Jesus was the great devotee and champion of "things religious," religious people still remember him with gratitude in their own new experiences, as the one who went before them. That is precisely why we project our own new experiences of God back on to Jesus. . . . Yet this says nothing whatever about Jesus of Nazareth himself, only something about our own new experiences.[23]

If a Christ of faith is to honor the claim that Christ is the presence of God, then there must be some sense in which the God in question is made known to us through Jesus Christ. If we already know that version of God independently of Jesus as the Christ and only subsequently claim Christ as a concrete exemplar of that God, then Christ becomes the presence of God in an extraordinarily attenuated sense. Thus, while the attractiveness of the panentheistic model of God, for example, might in many instances be the result of modern philosophical concerns and perspectives, the way in which this concept of God is filled in by the Christian theologians who employ it ought still to be a function of what is revealed in Jesus as the Christ.

At the same time, those radically christocentric theologies are naive that claim to derive their understanding of God wholly from what is shown in Jesus as the Christ. As Schillebeeckx admits, "Of course we have definite conceptions of . . . God, just as the Jews had when they encountered Jesus. Jesus himself stood within the tradition of the peculiar Yahwistic Jewish experience of God. This already given understanding is in no sense disavowed."[24] The Christ may deepen, or even overturn, these preexisting conceptions, but they must be present as a point of contact for the claim that Jesus Christ is the presence of God. Even in the case of our notion of God, then, the aforementioned christological circle comes into play: the contemporary world will alter our conceptions of deity, offering new possibilities for conceiving God, but Christians will ever come back to the Christ in order to, in turn, reformulate such new conceptions.

Providential and Nonprovidential Christs

If each of these notions of God—from God as supernatural personal agent to the enacted deity of some feminist religious consciousness—is operative in the contemporary pluralistic scene, then pictures of Christ as the presence of God can draw upon any of them. And we must keep in mind that there are innumerable variations possible upon each of these models. Such possibilities lead us up to the distinction between *providential* and *nonprovidential* Christs. The notion of nonprovidential Christs will further our exploration of christological pluralism, first of all, and most generally, simply because it adds another category of Christ to the discussion. Secondly, insofar as nonprovidential Christs will more readily be linked with contemporary, radically nonmetaphysical concepts of God than with older and more familiar God-concepts, a consideration of the notion of nonprovidential Christs will underscore the manner in which new ideas of God bring yet more Christs to birth. Finally, we shall see that nonprovidential Christs have a special link to christological pluralism inasmuch as they make possible the existence of contradictory, but genuine, Christs.

A providential Christ is one understood, as in traditional Christian doctrine, as the result of the initiative of a self-conscious deity. In other words, it is not merely that human beings do, as it turns out, happen to see God in Jesus of Nazareth, or even just that Jesus lives in such a way that some persons inevitably encounter God in him. Rather, God has decided to reveal himself definitively in Jesus.[25] There can be only one incarnation of God in Jesus, of course. But we can still talk about numerous providential Christs, insofar as there have been, and will no doubt continue to be, many different imaginative Christs of faith that are intended as responses to this providential incarnation.

A genuine but nonprovidential Christ is one that does make God present for its adherents, but does so independently of any self-conscious divine initiative. There need be nothing willful about this; devotees of a nonprovidential Christ do not simply decide to see God in Jesus Christ. Rather, there are actual characteristics of Jesus, and actual features of his acceptance as the Christ by earlier generations of Christians, that make it possible for him to be the presence of God for contemporary persons. At the same time, it is probably true that followers of a nonprovidential Christ will more readily acknowledge the large degree of imaginative construction involved in any Christ of faith than will followers of a providential Christ. Consider two reasons for this difference. First, there is no suggestion in the nonprovidential case of a supernatural, miraculous revelation over against which one might be largely passive, like Saint Paul knocked off his horse on the road to Damascus. Rather, it will be evident from the start that one must make some effort in order to recognize Jesus Christ as the presence of God. Second, nonprovidential Christs will tend to go together with notions of God that suggest that God itself is a function of human being, to a greater or lesser extent.[26]

Providential Christs and the model of God as a personal consciousness, a supernatural agent who stands outside the world but can intervene in it, fit together according to the dictates of ancient Christian doctrine. God as supernatural personal agent providentially decides to reveal himself by taking on flesh; the second person of the Trinity becomes incarnate in Jesus of Nazareth. This incarnation of the infinite in the finite would be a fact even if no human being were to recognize and respond to it, though it would not constitute a successful revelation in that case. When persons do faithfully respond to this divine initiative, the result is imaginary Christs, in the sense described in chapter 1.

In the clearest contrast to this scenario, the model of God that I have attributed above to Rosemary Radford Ruether and Carol Christ seems obviously to demand a nonprovidential view of Christ. If the divine is to be understood not as a self-conscious being, but as a relation that we must enact, even though it radically transcends us in some respects, then the fact that some persons encounter the divine in various versions of Jesus as the Christ cannot be read as a function of divine initiative in any ordinary sense.

While providential and nonprovidential Christs exist side-by-side within the contemporary pluralistic Christian milieu, they are of course, strictly speaking, inconsistent with one another. If there exists a God who is a personal consciousness, and if that God has decided to become incarnate in the man Jesus as a definitive self-revelation, then persons who think in terms of nonprovidential Christs are simply mistaken. On the other hand, if some people really do encounter God in various forms of Jesus as the Christ, but God has never made any decision to manifest Godself in a special way in Jesus, or is of such a nature that she cannot make decisions at all, then persons who think in terms of providential Christs are mistaken.

What are the most important differences that follow from embracing a nonprovidential rather than a providential Christ? Assuming that belief in a nonprovidential Christ is a function of embracing a model of God in which God is not a personal consciousness, a nonprovidential version of Christ probably cannot be understood to have been raised from the dead in anything like the literal sense.[27] There is no supernatural consciousness who can decide to raise him and intervene in the natural causal order. There are similar implications for the traditional doctrine of the ascension of Christ and for his role as second person of the Trinity.

But there are also some less obvious differences. First, the nonprovidentialist view suggests that, while Christs can never be entirely independent of Jesus of Nazareth, neither are they limited to the figure of Jesus. If there is no conscious divine decision to become incarnate in a wholly unique way in Jesus, then it is possible for the revelation in Jesus as the Christ to be instantiated in other places, though these will necessarily hearken back to Jesus as their starting point if they are still to be considered christic revelations.[28]

Second, the nonprovidential interpretation of Christs of faith allows for the existence of contradictory Christs in a way that the providentialist interpretation does not. Some Christs may be different from one another, but ultimately complementary. For example, my Christ of faith may emphasize Christ as the one who saves from personal sin while yours focuses on Christ as liberator from social injustice. Yet both views may be seen as perfectly legitimate, though distinct, responses to the same reality of Jesus as the Christ. But surely there are other Christs that cannot be so reconciled. For instance, suppose that your Christ of faith construes the Christ as one who demands pacifism from his followers, but mine construes the Christ as commanding the kind of "ethnic cleansing" directed by Christians against Muslims in the former Yugoslavia after the collapse of the Soviet Union, a program that entailed massive violence. These two Christs are simply irreconcilable. In this particular instance, however, it is to be hoped that both the providentialist and the nonprovidentialist interpretations can reject the second Christ as illegitimate. They ought to be able to do so using the very criterion now under discussion, namely, Christ as the presence of God. All of the models of God to which we have made reference provide grounds for unmasking the project of ethnic cleansing as all-too-human.

But now consider a more complicated scenario. Suppose that we found ourselves in Europe or the United States back in the period of Hitler's rise to power in Germany and subsequent assault upon Europe. One Christ of faith demands pacifism from his followers, while another suggests that it is necessary to take up arms against an evil such as Nazism. I decide one way, and you another. It may be that, if God is properly conceived as lacking anything akin to personal consciousness— recall that nonprovidential Christs accompany such a view—then there is no one right decision. Perhaps, in other words, there is nothing about the character of such a God and the way that God is revealed in Christ that makes one of these reactions to Nazism superior to the other. It is not simply that we cannot *know* which reaction more consistently follows from a life lived in harmony with God. Rather, there is nothing about God even in Godself that favors the one reaction over the other.

If we now switch to the model of God as a personal consciousness (whether in the older supernaturalistic sense or in panentheistic terms), while the situation will not necessarily be different, it clearly could be different. In other words, while it is conceivable that the self-conscious deity incarnate in Jesus of Nazareth could be indifferent about whether Christians take the one approach to Nazism or the other, or that he could see both approaches as somehow reflecting his will, would it not also be possible, and probably even likely, that he would in fact favor one option over the other? In the latter case, then, it is not true to say that two contradictory Christs are equally genuine. Even if both of the Christians in our example are equally pleasing to God, both having morally wrestled with the choice facing them and having come to the best interpretation of Christ available to them given their own abilities and situations, one interpretation still reflects the will of God, while the other does not.

Thus, while different persons who hold a providentialist view of Christs of faith can and do come up with contradictory Christs, they will maintain that when two Christs actually contradict one another, they cannot both be genuine Christs. This will be the case even in those situations where it is not possible for human beings to determine which Christs are in fact genuine and which are not. By contrast, persons who take the nonprovidentialist view can allow for the possibility that two contradictory Christs can both be genuine. Hence, the category of nonprovidential Christs adds to the contemporary pluralism of Christs not just in the obvious sense that it is a category of Christs in addition to the providential, but also because it multiplies genuine Christs by accepting this possibility of two contradictory Christs both being genuine.

Nonprovidential Christs and the Quest for Objectivity

None of this implies, of course, that a commitment to the notion of nonprovidential Christs leaves one without any means to sift through the multitude of Christs and reject some of them. Put differently, it does not imply that to embrace the idea of nonprovidential Christs is to be left without any way to distinguish between versions of Christ that are purely subjective projections and those that have a measure of objectivity. First of all, the very matter that we are in the midst of exploring in this chapter, that is, criteria that we can ask any version of Christ to address, is as applicable to nonprovidential Christs as to providential.

That is, we can attempt to sort through nonprovidential Christs of faith and reject those that we deem to inadequately address the three criteria of family resemblance with New Testament Christs, Christ as God, and Christ as source of redemption. Recall our example of being able to reject a Christ who would sanction ethnic cleansing.

Furthermore, there are some ways in which, if one grants the presuppositions of the nonprovidentialist view, nonprovidential Christs appear to possess greater objectivity over against their adherents than providential Christs do. Consider the issue of transcendence, for example. As the nonprovidentialist sees things, there is no such reality as a providential Christ. Hence, the notion of God as a personal consciousness choosing to become incarnate in the man Jesus is, if taken literally, a projection of human attributes onto the divine. As such, it is bound to misperceive the genuine character of divine transcendence. The nonprovidential interpretation obviously avoids this particular difficulty. Furthermore, precisely because of its unambiguous recognition of the fact that Christ-formation is not a matter of passively receiving divine revelation, but, rather, involves a large measure of imaginative construction, the nonprovidential interpretation may better equip one to respect divine transcendence. In other words, we find ourselves back at the transcendence paradox. It is by recognizing the human, limited character of our categories that we enable those categories to point us to the divine. Without such recognition, the categories become instruments of projection that hide the transcendent. But when their limitations are faced, we are in a better position to avoid projection and thus to allow the transcendent to show itself both through and in spite of those categories.[29]

There is yet another way in which nonprovidential Christs can avoid the pitfall of mere subjectivity and projection. Let us take Rosemary Radford Ruether's christology as an example here. Ruether perceives the divine, or God/ess—a reality that transcends the gender categories suggested by the terms "god" and "goddess"—as the Primal Matrix. The Primal Matrix is the encompassing source of all that is, a reality both transcendent and immanent.[30] I have indicated above that Ruether's theological vision can fruitfully be read in terms of the enactment model of divinity. But whether it is understood that way or, less controversially perhaps, as closer to Tillich's deliberations about God as being-itself, it seems a vision consistent with the notion of nonprovidential Christs.

As has already been noted, one possible characteristic of nonprovidential Christs is that, while they can never be entirely independent of Jesus of Nazareth—connection with Jesus has always been part of the notion of Christ and hence constitutes a portion of the objective identity of Christs of faith—neither are they limited to the figure of Jesus. Ruether openly embraces this possibility: "While Jesus is the foundational representative of this way of the cross and liberation, he is not its exclusive possibility."[31] Drawing on the tradition of spirit christologies, she goes on to make the provocative suggestion that we should see Christ in the form of our sisters and brothers.[32] Actual persons around us within the community of faith, and perhaps in the larger human community, exemplify and continue what Ruether calls "Christic personhood."[33] This decision to focus on the ongoing reality of Christ in contemporary persons is thoroughly consistent with the distinction between the Jesus of history and the Christ of faith. She writes,

> Christ, as redemptive person and Word of God, is not to be encapsulated "once-for-all" in the historical Jesus. The Christian community continues Christ's identity. As vine and branches Christic personhood continues in our sisters and brothers. In the language of early Christian prophetism, we can encounter Christ *in the form of our sister*. Christ, the liberated humanity, is not confined to a static perfection of one person two thousand years ago. Rather, redemptive humanity goes ahead of us, calling us to yet incompleted dimensions of human liberation.[34]

Indeed, the distinction between the Jesus of history and the ongoing, present-day Christ of faith is particularly important for feminist Christian thinkers, inasmuch as it can show the relative unimportance of Jesus' maleness: the male Jesus of history is only one part of the larger reality of the Christ. Not surprisingly, then, other feminist religious thinkers echo Ruether's point. Rita Nakashima Brock argues, for example, that "for both love and justice to exist, there must be more than one person, no matter how spectacular he may be. For the power of God as love to be fully incarnate, the full presence of God cannot reside in Jesus only, but in the messy middle of our relationships."[35] In other words, Christians claim that Jesus is the paradigmatic instantiation of God's love and justice. But love and justice are, by their very nature, relational phenomena: one cannot be said to manifest love and justice by oneself, in isolation from one's relationships with other beings. Thus, in order to encounter the fullness of God's love, we must look not just to Jesus, but to Jesus and other persons besides.

What is relevant here about the nonprovidentialist claim that Christ is manifest in other persons is that these christic sisters and brothers contribute an element of otherness to our perceptions of the Christ, an otherness that can help to check tendencies toward mere projection in our Christs of faith. Of course, it is up to us to choose which persons we shall regard as representatives of christic personhood. Furthermore, we will inevitably attempt to project our expectations and prejudices upon them. But the otherness of these other persons can often show through nonetheless and in some cases can even change those expectations and prejudices. In order to see how this happens, one need not retreat from contemporary hermeneutical theory and embrace Plato's preference for speech over writing. The other is a kind of text for me, in that I interpret him or her. Yet the other can act back upon my reading in a way that a written text cannot. But this is not simply because the other can correct my misinterpretations of his or her meaning via face-to-face dialogue.

Let us consider three ways in which the other person has greater otherness over against my reading than does a written text. The "New Hermeneuts" used to like to talk about the text interpreting the reader.[36] But the multitude of different Christs of faith that readers find grounding for in the New Testament suggests that this claim is, at the very least, highly problematic. The reader can apparently always block the text from interpreting him or her. But I as reader can never stop the other person from reading me. This is engagingly illustrated in Italo Calvino's novel, *If on a winter's night a traveler,* in which the protagonist constantly reads his lover. But then Calvino reminds his protagonist, with whom we are identified as we read the novel: "And you, too, O Reader, are meanwhile an object of reading: the Other Reader is now reviewing your body as if skimming the index."[37] If one's imaginative construction of a Christ of faith includes reading certain sisters and brothers as exemplars of christic personhood, one cannot stop those others from reading the reader in turn.

Second, the other person has a moral claim over against me and my reading of him or her. A written text may constitute a moral claim on the basis of some content that it presents, but the other person has a moral claim upon me by his or her very existence. The other is the insistent presence of a moral demand that always challenges my reading of him or her. Of course, to see the other as presenting this moral demand is perhaps itself a function of my reading of the other, but it is nonetheless a different matter from how one approaches the reading of a text, as Emmanuel Levinas' quasi-phenomenological analysis of human otherness helps to clarify.[38]

Third, a written text and the human other have different temporal structures. While I can of course come back to a text over and over again and find new meaning each time, so that the text is in a sense never finished, this is, at least in part, a function of the different horizons that interpreters can bring to the text. Where the human other is concerned, by contrast, the object of my reading remains, during his or her lifetime, unfinished in a more profound sense. The freedom of the other person means that he or she can move in wholly unexpected directions, perhaps even reversing course from time to time, and this is totally independent of how the interpretive horizons that are brought to the other may change or remain the same. Thus, there is a peculiar way in which my reading of the other can never encompass him or her, since the temporal horizon of this other's being is always wider than the horizon of my here-and-now act of consciousness within which I attempt to place the other.

If, as Ruether suggests, Christ is not limited to the man Jesus, but is to be found in particular contemporary sisters and brothers, then there is a potential measure of protection against my Christ of faith being simply my own subjective projection. For the concrete otherness of those sisters and brothers can call into question my prejudices and predilections. That otherness is manifest in my christic sisters' and brothers' ability to read me even as I read them, in their moral demand upon me, and in how their being escapes my attempts to cognitively encompass it.

It would appear, then, that the notion of nonprovidential Christs does not necessitate resigning oneself to the idea that imaginary Christs of faith can be nothing more than arbitrary subjective constructions. On the contrary, the nonprovidentialist can still sort through the multitude of Christs of faith by asking each Christ to address certain criteria, such as the criterion at issue here, namely, that Christ is God. He or she can argue that, thanks especially to the transcendence paradox, nonprovidential Christs can effectively confront one with a transcendent dimension of reality. And the nonprovidentialist can point to an example such as Ruether's christology, with its claim that we can see Christ in our sisters and brothers, to show that there are potential checks against a Christ of faith that is merely a subjective projection.

None of this is intended or expected to convince the reader that the nonprovidentialist position is superior to the providentialist one. The choice of one position over the other will most likely be based upon one's already existing convictions about the character of the divine. Rather, the arguments that I have adduced here are simply meant to suggest that the nonprovidentialist reading of Christs of faith has a consistent internal logic and deserves to be taken seriously. If the nonprovidential interpretation is in fact taken seriously and allowed to take its place beside the providential one, this will serve to reinforce our sense of the expansive pluralism that characterizes the contemporary christological scene.

Christ is God: The Criterion in Action

This whole discussion of providential and nonprovidential Christs falls under the heading of our exploration of the criterion that Christ must somehow be understood as the presence of God. Before leaving our exploration of that criterion, we need to think briefly about how the criterion has in fact operated in the larger christological discussion of the modern and contemporary eras. One might initially think of the criterion as being little more than tautological where the Christian tradition is concerned: a Christian is one who believes that Jesus Christ is the presence of God; if one holds that Jesus Christ is anything less, he or she is simply not a Christian. But that would be a simplistic reading. While it is certainly true that nothing has been more definitive of the Christian faith than the claim that Jesus is in some sense the presence of God, there have been extraordinary pressures brought to bear on that claim in the modern and postmodern eras, and it is easy to find powerful examples of the modern and contemporary struggle over Jesus as God.

Consider just three examples. In a letter written in 1822, that paragon of Enlightenment rationality, Thomas Jefferson, exclaimed, "I confidently expect that the present generation will see Unitarianism become the general religion of the United States." Jefferson endorsed Unitarianism over what he regarded as "the hocus-pocus phantasm of a God like another Cerberus, with one body and three heads."[39] A Unitarian is, of course, one who rejects the doctrine of the Trinity, and thus denies that Jesus was God. Jefferson was a Deist, and the rejection of Trinitarian Christianity is part and parcel of the rationalist approach to religion espoused by Deism. But Jefferson, like so many other Westerners suspicious of traditional Christian dogma, did not wish to get rid of Jesus himself. Indeed, in a letter to a friend he averred, "I am a Christian, in the only sense he wished anyone to be; sincerely attached to his doctrines, in preference to all others; ascribing to himself every human excellence; and believing he never claimed any other."[40] The "doctrine" of which Jefferson speaks approvingly is Jesus' moral teaching, to which Jefferson essentially reduced Jesus' significance, a fact evident in his remarkable *The Life and Morals of Jesus of Nazareth*.[41] That work, which Jefferson had contemplated for several years but probably completed around 1820, consisted in an abridgement of the four gospels that removed all of what Jefferson regarded as fallacious dogma and preserved Jesus' ethical message.[42] Jefferson started with four editions of the gospels, one in Greek, a second in Latin, a third in French, and a fourth in English. He then clipped out the parallel sections from each edition that he took to be the authentic teachings of Jesus and pasted them side-by-side. The Jeffersonian Jesus that results from this confident bit of editing tells us how God would have us live our lives, but he cannot himself be equated with God.

Jefferson was not the only American intellectual to launch a nineteenth-century assault upon the divinity of Jesus. Ralph Waldo Emerson created an uproar when he delivered his famous address to the Harvard Divinity School in July of 1838, in which he ridiculed Christian orthodoxy's version of the claim that Jesus was divine. It is not Jesus' person that ought to be emphasized, argued Emerson, but rather his grasp of the beauty of the human soul, and his message that God can become incarnate in any person who opens up his soul in the way that Jesus did. For Emerson himself, "If a man is at heart just, then in so far is he God."[43] Christ is not absolutely unique in this regard. Historical Christianity dwells, Emerson charged, "with noxious exaggeration about the person of Jesus."[44] All of this is consistent, of course, with Emerson's emphasis upon selfhood: "That is always best which gives me to myself. . . . That which shows God in me, fortifies me. That which shows God out of me, makes me a wart and a wen."[45] Jesus may manifest the presence of God, but only in a fashion to which others too can, and should, aspire.

The attempt to hold onto Jesus while casting off the orthodox claim that he is God is repeated yet again in the twentieth century. A notable example is provided by the notorious "death-of-God" theology of the 1960s. Among the several loosely allied thinkers associated with that movement, Paul van Buren provides perhaps the clearest statement of the idea that one can have Christian commitment to Jesus without believing that Jesus is God, indeed without speaking of God at all. According to the dramatic analysis of the contemporary situation in van Buren's book, *The Secular Meaning of the Gospel*, "Today, we cannot even understand the Nietzschian cry that 'God is dead!' for if it were so, how could we know? No, the problem now is that the *word* 'God' is dead."[46] But despite the need to embrace an empirical rather than a metaphysical approach to Christianity today, we can still understand Jesus in terms that do justice to his transformative effect upon those who follow him. It is Jesus' freedom that is central for van Buren's interpretation of the effect of the gospel upon us: "in response to the proclamation of the free man who has set men free the hearer finds himself to some extent set free."[47]

What is significant, first of all, about these three examples is that they remind us of the pressure that has been constantly brought to bear upon the traditional Christian understanding of God throughout the modern and contemporary periods. Each thinker seeks a way to hold up Jesus of Nazareth while distancing himself from the history of Christian God-talk. Jefferson seeks to do so through the Enlightenment rationalism of his day, Emerson through his own version of nineteenth-century Romanticism, and van Buren by utilizing the tools of twentieth-century Anglo-American linguistic analysis. What is more, each of these attempts had a significant degree of power and saliency in its own day.

Jefferson was one of the towering intellectual figures of his epoch. Emerson too possessed a rare genius, and the sort of religious Romanticism he espoused still exercises an influence, in however diluted and generalized a form, on contemporary American consciousness. The death-of-God theology, of which van Buren's book is one instance, may not belong in the same company as Jefferson and Emerson. Indeed, theologians of a more traditional bent could denounce it at the time, albeit a bit defensively, as "either nonsense, trivial, naive, or pathetic."[48] Still, the death of God movement in theology captured the public attention for a time during the 1960s in a way that few other theological discussions have done in the contemporary period.

But what is most interesting for our purposes here is that, despite the power of these proposals and their seeming consonance with the sensibilities of their eras, none of them ever took root in American Christianity. The criterion that Jesus must be understood as God, at least in some fashion, appears to have been operative in the larger dynamic of Christian consciousness in such a way as to render these christological proposals unappealing. Of course one could interpret the same evidence differently: perhaps many persons were in fact influenced by proposals of the sort cited here. To the extent that they decided to embrace a Jesus who bore no marks of divinity, they were simply no longer Christians and abandoned their connections with the church. Thus, we cannot really conclude anything about the operative power of the criterion that Jesus must be the presence of God.

Or, to take another tack that undermines the apparent power of the criterion that Jesus is the presence of God, one might return to some of the negative interpretations mentioned earlier. Suppose that the desire to see Christ as God is a function of an anxious craving for a secure hold upon salvation, a flight from finitude, or an expression of a triumphalist mentality. In that case, the Christian resistance to the kinds of proposals set forth by Jefferson, Emerson, and van Buren represents not the powerful influence within the Christian community of a healthy christological criterion but, rather, evidence of Christians' inability to overcome their neuroses.

My decision to interpret the evidence as pointing to the perfectly healthy effect of the criterion that Christ is the presence of God is a result of my sense that the desire for transcendence that the criterion represents is itself a healthy and desirable element of the human condition. Despite postmodern attacks upon the notion of "human nature," the historical record seems to suggest that the majority of persons in all times and cultures have desired to live, as Peter Berger puts it, in a "world with windows," that is, a world that opens out upon the transcendent.[49] Of course the transcendent can be conceived in innumerable ways, some of which we have briefly considered by looking at a number of basic models of God. Thus, to hold to the criterion that Jesus is the very presence of God, while it will cut against some Christs of faith, still allows for many different imaginary Christs. The Christ who is the providential incarnation of a God conceived as a supernatural personal consciousness is significantly different, for example, from a Christ who incarnates a God or Goddess understood as a relation that human beings can aspire to enact.

THE CHRIST PROVIDES REDEMPTION

The verb "redeem" comes from the Latin *redimere*, which means "to buy back." In its classical Christian usage, the notion of redemption suggests that human beings have become enslaved by sin and must be redeemed in the sense of having their freedom bought back for them by God in Christ. Both this vocabulary and the concepts it attempts to express will strike many contemporary ears as antiquated. Yet it has been the nearly universal testimony of the world's religions that human existence is somehow out of joint. The Noble Truths taught by the Buddha explain that life is suffering, and that we must seek a way beyond the illusions that cause suffering. In the Hindu or Indian religious traditions, human beings are pictured as bound to the wheel of *saṃsāra*, a cycle of redeath. According to the Taoist sages, we are mired in a counterproductive attitude of calculation and resistance to the way of the universe. Both the Jewish and the Muslim traditions concern themselves with our propensity to fall short of our responsibilities toward God and our fellow human beings.

As is the case with Judaism and Islam, Christian faith focuses upon human responsibility to God and others. But traditional Christian thought has been particularly severe about how far short we fall of those responsibilities. Indeed, from its perspective our existence is profoundly colored by the fallenness of the whole human race, a fallenness that is the result of our rebellion against God.

The Decentering of the Self

The very notion of responsibility to God and my neighbor, the idea that I know the difference between good and evil and ought to do the good, may appear to entail the notion of a centered self. That is, if I am to be held responsible for the ethical decisions I make, then it must be fully within my power to make the right decision. If I were merely the plaything of external forces, it would be unreasonable to hold me responsible for my actions. Thus, it seems that the self, rather than being simply a chaos of conflicting tendencies, must possess a unifying center that can react to the various forces that impinge upon it, a center out of which it can issue decisions that transcend any one of those forces.

Yet the contemporary age is characterized by numerous powerful attempts to decenter the self. A variety of intellectual movements have conspired to convince us that the self is not securely centered after all. It is in large part thanks to these movements, and the new perspectives that they inspire, that we are justified in talking of a transition from the modern age to the postmodern.

The assault upon the centered self finds one of its most important early representatives in Sigmund Freud. His work seeks to convince us that, rather than being our own master, each of us is subject to unconscious forces that powerfully motivate our behavior. Thus, our decisions often flow, not from some unifying center of consciousness, but from hidden recesses of the larger psyche, recesses that harbor potent desires and drives that may remain largely opaque even after we are made aware of their existence. The self is decentered not only in the sense that the wellspring of its behavior is often hidden in the unconscious rather than safely ensconced in a perfectly autonomous and translucent self-consciousness, but also insofar as the conflict between our desires and society's rules and regulations often pushes the psyche off-center and into neuroses. Freudian psychoanalysis has not fared well in scientific studies of its effectiveness as a treatment for psychological ills. But as a description of our condition, rather than a technique for its healing, Freud's theories continue to exercise a hold on much contemporary thinking.

Influential currents in contemporary philosophy have followed Freud's lead in reading the self as decentered. Most notably, those philosophical positions loosely allied under the rubric "poststructuralism" have emphasized that the meanings in terms of which we live are not the creations and secure possessions of individual subjects. The subject is itself a function of intersecting linguistic forces, rather than the one who wields those forces in order to bring meaning to birth. Hence all meanings, especially those communicated in writing, escape the subjective intention of the subject. It is this phenomenon that provides the opening for deconstructive readings of a text.

If practitioners of the natural sciences have been highly suspicious of the positions advanced by Freudians and by champions of deconstructionist, postmodern theory, they have exerted pressures of their own upon the notion of the centered self. Advances in our understanding of the brain, for instance, have made it clear to some that consciousness is wholly a function of physical brain processes. Thus, who we are and what we do appear to come down, in large part, to electrochemical processes in our brain tissue, rather than to the deliberations of some physically unencumbered spiritual center of the self. This means that, to cite a practical example, some scientists now hold that even a matter such as our sexual preference, which once appeared to be paradigmatic instance of an ethical choice by a free personal center of consciousness, may in fact be biologically determined.

Nor do things look much better for the centered self if we push the "nurture" side of the now-familiar "nature-versus-nurture" debate. Suppose, in other words, that we grant an important role to biology in determining our identity and behavior, but then go on to argue that an even more significant factor in determining the kind of persons we shall end up being is how we are affected by our environment. For instance, while my brain chemistry is an important starting point, how my parents raised me may have an even greater role to play in determining my identity. But this scenario too, at least in its most potent formulations, seems to take responsibility away from a personal center, locating it instead in forces outside the self.[50]

Even the conquest of our society by the computer has implications for our understanding of selfhood. While artificial intelligence is still a contentious issue among computer scientists and philosophers, the very possibility that a computer may someday be able to think in a way indistinguishable from how human beings think, raises profound questions about the nature of the self. If it turns out that our thought processes, including our ability to make decisions, can be mirrored by feeding a set of mathematically coded instructions into a construction of silicone chips and wire, what are the implications for the notion of an autonomous personal center? Would we conclude that a thinking computer has a personal center, or would the advent of genuine artificial intelligence strike one more blow against the concept of the centered self?

Can the traditional Christian claim that human beings require redemption, presupposing as it apparently does some sense of personal responsibility, coexist with contemporary notions of the decentered self? The traditional Christian concept (or concepts) of the self may not be as dependent on the notion of centerdness as one might first assume. The Christian concept of selfhood is, after all, a complex one. It is a concept that emphasizes the conflicted character of the self. Hence Paul's cry of desperation: "I do not understand my own actions. For I do not do what I want, but I do the very thing I hate. . . . I can will what is right, but I cannot do it. . . . Now if I do what I do not want, it is no longer I that do it, but sin that dwells within me." (Romans 7:15; 18b; 20) There are elements of centeredness here—the ability to consistently will what is right, for example—as well as suggestions that the self is decentered— the sense that it is not I who act.

The Centered Self, the Decentered Self,
and Classical Christian Notions of Justification

This view of the self as conflicted, which holds in tension the self as centered with the self as decentered, provides yet another opportunity for Christian pluralism. Different Christian concepts of the human condition and our need for redemption through the Christ can put differing degrees of emphasis on these two poles. One way in which to see how this is so is to consider an overly neat, but potentially helpful, schematism of classical Christian attitudes toward justification. While these attitudes will seem woefully out of date to many contemporary persons, Christians included, we go back to them here to get at the root of the pluralism that characterizes Christian thinking about the self and redemption. The concept of justification in this context means being put in a just relationship with God; it means being redeemed from the unjust relationship, the estrangement, created by one's sinful rebellion against God. Let us say that *forensic approaches to justification privilege a decentered view of the self but allow for a centered view*, while *transformationist approaches to justification privilege a centered view of the self but allow for a decentered view.*

In the forensic approach favored by the classical Lutheran tradition, justification consists in one's being declared just by God even though one in fact remains a sinner. Rather than one's inner nature being transformed, in other words, one's "legal" status before God is simply altered, hence the term "forensic." To put the matter in the peculiarly American terms of a contemporary gospel song, "Jesus dropped the charges." Such redemption really does alter one's existence, of course. For instance, it is a prerequisite for entry into eternal life with God. But, due to this position's firm convictions about the power of sin, it expects very little from the human person. Everything rests with the grace of God.

This version of justification can be read as privileging a view of the fallen self as decentered in that it regards any personal center in the self as having been so corrupted by sin that it has been rendered inoperative. Perhaps the self as created by God, in its original goodness, was in fact centered, but the Fall into sin has pushed the self off-center. As a result, the self is now beholden to sundry forces and temptations that come its way from without. In this model, redemption too comes wholly from the outside, that is, by grace alone, *sola gratia.*

The secondary way of reading the forensic approach, however, would be to emphasize the centeredness of the self and to say that the Fall means that sin has captured one's personal center. In other words, it is not that the self after the Fall is without a center and is whipsawed by countless external forces, but that the self's fully intact center is now in bondage to sin.[51] Our acts of will are quite consistent and serve to unify our character. The problem is that we will to do evil. Here too, of course, the self is impotent to heal itself, and the prescription for recovery is the same: the wholly unmerited grace of God that is received through faith in Jesus Christ.

The transformationist attitude toward justification is one that thinks of justification as entailing an actual transformation of one's behavior toward God and others. Thus, this model differs from the forensic one by tending to place justification in greater proximity to what the tradition calls "sanctification," the process through which one becomes capable of living a holy life. In the view set forth in the sixteenth century by the Roman Catholic Council of Trent as a response to the Reformation, for example, justification is accomplished by the individual's will working in cooperation with God's offer of grace in Christ. Thus, this approach to justification assumes that the will, while it may have been weakened by sin, is still intact. And it suggests that, rather than God simply declaring the believer just while he or she is in fact still a sinner, the believer actually moves away from the life of sin.

The transformationist view of justification, then, easily can be read as privileging the view that the self is centered. For here the self is apparently not buffeted about by external forces, but is fully able to decide, out of a defining center of its being, to accept the offer of divine grace and work in harmony with God.

But a secondary reading is possible in this case too. Suppose we go back to the version of the transformationist approach represented by Augustine in his fight with Pelagianism. Augustine did not think of justification in forensic terms. Rather, he held that justification meant an actual transformation of the self in its behavior. Yet that transformation was not accomplished by a decision that the self made out of a free personal center, in cooperation with the grace of God. Instead, Augustine viewed the transformation as wholly the work of grace: God empowered the person to live a new life, quite independently of anything that the person could will to do on his or her own. In this instance, the transformationist approach is rendered potentially compatible with a view of the self as decentered.[52] For now one might say that decisions are in fact not made out of some personal center, but that the self and its decisions are beholden to forces that energize it from without. For those predestined by God to salvation, the operative force is the divine grace that empowers one to live a righteous life.

The Relational Self

This schematism suggests a plurality of possible Christian views on the self and its need for redemption through the Christ. There are two fundamental models of justification, each of which can, in turn, be read in at least two different ways. But there are significant limitations in this quick overview. First of all, talk about the will being in bondage to sin, for example, may well be unintelligible to many contemporary persons, and it might even be regarded as destructive, as I mentioned earlier by reference to feminist complaints about the traditional Christian emphasis upon sin. Second, any superficial treatment of centeredness tends to suggest that the centered self, if not a windowless monad, is nonetheless a relatively self-contained entity. Suppose that we opt now for a concept of the self as relational. Here we can borrow Heidegger's famous formulation of human being as "being-in-the-world."[53] The self is what it is precisely through its relationships with what it encounters in the world round about it. The relational notion does not narrow the options for Christian thought about the self, for now the discussion about centerdness and decentering simply begins all over again on another level. One can read a relational model of selfhood as suggesting that the self's moving outside itself to enact relations with what is other, is a dynamic that arises out of its personal center and through which the self attains its essential being. Or one can conclude that the self is always decentered, constantly attempting to find itself in purely contingent and precarious syntheses of the "here" of the body and the many "theres" of its relations.

This relational view of selfhood affords the opportunity to broaden the concept of sin and redemption. For if the very being of the self is to be found in its relations with what is other, then the self, its fallenness, and its redemption will necessarily be tied up with the larger structures in which the self participates. Thus, we are in a position to see beyond purely individualistic notions of sin to the emphasis in much contemporary Christian theology on social sin. Reinhold Niebuhr, for example, already pointed to the way in which basically moral individuals create sinful social structures.[54] And contemporary theologies of liberation highlight political and economic oppression as forms of sin that the Christ seeks to overturn.

Consider the pluralism that now confronts us. There can now be christologies that focus on liberation from structures of oppression, as well as christologies that focus on liberation from personal sin. This means, furthermore, that there can be christologies that concentrate on the need for redemption from a bondage for which one is not responsible, as in most liberation theologies, as well as christologies that still concentrate on the need for redemption from one's own sinful behavior, whether purely personal or a function of one's participation in sinful social structures.

We can ask already at this point whether these various options are all mutually exclusive. Liberation theology will necessarily emphasize the redemption of innocent victims. Does it have no place, then, for the notion of redemption from one's own sin? It could conceivably find two different places for that traditional emphasis. First, to the extent that a liberation theology successfully addresses not just the victims of oppression but also those who benefit from oppressive structures, it will point to Christ as the one who can redeem us from the sin of contributing to oppression. Second, while the victims of oppression must never be blamed for that oppression, as human beings they are nonetheless subject to moral shortcomings of other kinds. Redemption from sin is required at this point too. Of course, even these shortcomings may be affected by the oppressed persons' situation of oppression. This suggests that moral responsibility and sin are contextual, not in the sense that different moral principles apply in different situations, but in that different levels of responsibility and degrees of moral culpability follow from the different social circumstances in which human beings find themselves. Thus, we may reasonably expect that there will be a number of different imaginary Christs bringing redemption to persons in these diverse circumstances.

The notion that different kinds of redemption will be required in different circumstances, whether the differences be individual or social, is behind the "method of correlation" employed by some theologians. Already in the work of the Jewish philosopher Hermann Cohen, founder of Marburg Neo-Kantianism, one finds the insight that "the relation between God and man proves itself to be a *correlation*."[55] The divine is never grasped purely in itself or for its own sake, but only in correlation with our particular sensibilities and needs, as our reflections on the role of imagination in the formation of Christs has already suggested. Paul Tillich turns this insight about the correlative character of all our talk about the divine into a theological method.[56] He shows how a philosophical analysis of the particular cultural and existential situation in which human beings find themselves can uncover the fundamental questions for which those persons seek answers. The Christian message, says Tillich, must then be articulated in such a way that it can be seen to offer the answers to these existential questions. David Tracy has offered important clarifications to Tillich's account of correlation. As Tracy suggests, the questions and answers must be "mutually critical."[57] The philosophical analysis does not articulate the questions in isolation from the religious answers, nor are the answers articulated by a religious tradition without critical input from philosophical sources.

A correlational approach to articulating how the Christ provides redemption reinforces the recognition that christological pluralism is inevitable. Different forms of redemption will be necessary in different circumstances. To summarize the reasons for pluralism that we have uncovered in this section, then, we begin with the fact that the Christian notion of selfhood is a complex one. It attempts to hold in tension two poles, that is, the element of centeredness in the self and the decentering forces encountered by the self. In their search for redemption through the Christ, different christologies may put different degrees of emphasis on the two poles. Pluralism is enhanced again by the fact that redemption through the Christ can be thought of as addressing both personal sin and sinful social structures. And redemption may be sought both from forces over which I have no control and from sinful behavior for which I am responsible, whether simply as an individual or as part of a group.

The Christ Provides Redemption: The Criterion in Action

In the last section, on the criterion of Christ as the presence of God, we briefly considered how that criterion had been at work in modern Christian thought. What about the criterion that Christ provides redemption? We have seen that the notion of redemption through the Christ is subject to a wide variety of interpretations. And recall that we are not asking christologies to obey the criterion in some mechanical fashion, but only to address it. Can we find evidence, then, of christologies taking this criterion seriously even in the contemporary era, despite the fact that many persons in our era are suspicious of notions such as sin?

One fascinating modern episode in which theologians struggled with the claim that Christ must do more than simply teach or comfort us, that he must in some sense redeem us, is found in the controversy surrounding Norman Vincent Peale's staggeringly popular book *The Power of Positive Thinking*, which was first published in 1953. It is tempting to see that book as epitomizing the easy optimism of upper- and middle-class white society in America in the 1950s, though, as I suggested by reference to Robert Schuller in chapter 1, it is not without its advocates even today. Peale holds that a self-consciously nurtured positive mental outlook can cure a host of ills, from business problems to marital conflicts. He presents this program of positive thinking not so much as a way of life that defines one's being, but more as a tool at one's disposal. He is espousing "scientific yet simple principles of achievement, health, and happiness."[58] These are the "simple techniques of faith taught in the Bible."[59] Peale's language is often indistinguishable from contemporary New Age and self-help vocabulary, as when he explains, "it is my conviction that the principles of Christianity scientifically utilized can develop an uninterrupted and continuous flow of energy into the human mind and body."[60]

While Peale clearly sees this spiritual strategy as flowing from Jesus himself—it is a program given to us "by the greatest Teacher who ever lived and who still lives"—it is a version of Christian faith that seems to have little connection with classical notions of the cross and redemption.[61] Guilt, for example, is here not something to be confronted, but rather something to be put aside through proper spiritual hygiene: "The effect of guilt and fear feelings on energy is widely recognized by all authorities having to do with the problems of human nature."[62]

At the height of the book's popularity, professional theologians roundly criticized the version of faith in the Christ that Peale seemed to be advancing. In 1955, for example, Reinhold Niebuhr denounced the feel-good piety presented by Peale and others as "forms of self-worship." Jesus' "Repent ye, for the kingdom of heaven is at hand" was being reduced, according to Niebuhr, to the "power of positive thinking."[63] The sight of an erudite professional theologian such as Niebuhr taking on the popular preacher may appear to some as an unsavory exercise in condescension. Niebuhr is doing little more, so one might think, than pushing over a straw man as a kind of intellectual stretching exercise, in preparation for a more strenuous theological workout to be found somewhere else. But it seems to me that there is, in fact, more at issue here. Niebuhr is highlighting the criterion that the Christ must provide redemption. He is arguing that Peale's Christianity makes redemption seem much too simple a matter, and that redemption is, for Peale, ultimately something that we accomplish under our own power. Jesus has provided spiritual advice, and it is up to us to put that advice into practice in such a way as to free ourselves from negative thinking. All of this seems a far cry, Niebuhr suggests, from classical Christian notions of the power of sin and the role of Christ on the cross in our redemption. It is not necessary for our purposes here to decide whether Niebuhr's criticism is justified or whether the classical concepts of sin and redemption still make sense. Rather, the point is that the kind of response to Peale represented by Niebuhr's attack provides an example of the criterion of Christ as redeemer being applied in the modern christological discussion.

A more contemporary example of that criterion's presence is provided by theologies of liberation. Christian theologies of liberation, whether Latin American, African American, feminist, or womanist, turn to the figure of Jesus as the Christ as source of liberation. The liberation they seek may not be identical with what earlier Christian tradition has meant by redemption, but it is clearly a contemporary analogue. For here, too, Christ is said to set free, to "buy back," from a condition that did not obtain in God's good creation of the world and should not obtain in the present. Precisely because the redemption-as-liberation addressed by these theologies concerns such widely destructive and deep-rooted forces—economic exploitation, political tyranny, racism, sexism—redemption must be taken by these theologies with utmost seriousness. There is little chance, in other words, that theologies of liberation will let the claim that Christ is redeemer fade from view and put in its place a facile picture of Christ as the author of pithy self-help hints. The very fact that theologies of liberation have a high profile in contemporary Christian thought assures that the criterion of Christ as redeemer will remain alive in present-day christological discussion and struggle.

Let us briefly look back at the ground we have traversed in this chapter. We have suggested that, as a means of Christ-testing, every christology ought to be asked to address three criteria: family resemblance with the Christs of the New Testament, the claim that Christ is the presence of God, and the claim that Christ provides redemption. The actual process of employing these criteria will never be easy or unproblematic. For one thing, we have noted an extraordinary pluralism internal to each of the three criteria: each is interpreted in many different ways. And even if we were to settle upon one interpretation of a particular criterion, how would we decide just what constitutes "successfully addressing" that criterion?

But despite these difficulties, we can still discern a healthy process of Christ-testing going on here. The very arguments about different interpretations of the criteria and about how to apply them can be understood as part of this process. In other words, we can envision the process of Christ-testing as a vigorous conversation among the various vantage points on the criteria. And our examples of how the larger Christian community has rejected or severely criticized christologies perceived not to take the criteria seriously—recall our discussions of Jefferson, Emerson, the death-of-God theology, and Peale—indicate that the criteria are in fact at work in the modern and contemporary scene. It is important to note, however, that these examples are one-sided. They all illustrate a conservative dynamic, in which the larger tradition rejects imaginary Christs that appear not to address the criteria. But there is another possibility: might it not happen that the larger tradition is confronted with the fact, thanks to a challenge by a subtradition for example, that the criteria as applied in the present situation dictate an innovation in the church's christology? Is it not possible, in other words, that the criteria, in addition to their conservative function of blocking various christological proposals, can also demand changes in the christological thinking of the larger church? Liberation theology, cited as an example at the end of our exploration of redemption, provides an instance of this possibility. In the next chapter, we shall consider one form of liberation theology, namely, African American theology of liberation, and see how it illustrates the ability of a subtradition to direct the criterion of Christ as redeemer back upon the larger Christian tradition. This will help to fill out our understanding of what is involved in Christ-testing.

CHAPTER 4

Black Christs

The Christ provides redemption. Thus, any genuine imaginary Christ must make redemption available to his followers, or in some fashion address the problem of redemption. But the notion of redemption must be correlated with a particular situation. Even if Christians perennially think of redemption as the process through which our estrangement from God is overcome, there can be innumerable variations on the concepts "God," "estrangement," and even "overcome." How is redemption to be conceived, then, in contemporary American society?

Derrick Bell, in his provocative collection of essays, *Faces at the Bottom of the Well: The Permanence of Racism*, cites some devastating statistics about life in the United States: in 1990, approximately one out of every four young black men was either in prison or on parole or probation. In the District of Columbia in 1991, 42 percent of black men aged eighteen through thirty-five were under the jurisdiction of the criminal justice system.[1] How could these figures represent anything but a crisis for the society that has produced them? If the redemption of which Christian faith speaks is real, it cannot leave untouched such a profound moral and spiritual crisis, a crisis that confronts the entire society. If a Christ of faith has nothing to offer in the face of this suffering, then it has failed to address, let alone exemplify, the criterion that the Christ must provide redemption.

Since the 1960s, there has existed a vigorous black theology in the United States, a movement in Christian thought that begins from the experience of African Americans and interprets the gospel in terms of black persons' quest for liberation from racism and economic exploitation. This current of theology is sufficiently well defined and distinctive that we may usefully consider it a contemporary subtradition of the larger Christian tradition. As such, it has the potential to act back upon that larger tradition and shape its grasp of Christs of faith. Two effective advocates of contemporary black theology are James Cone, who is the best known of all its practitioners, and Jacquelyn Grant, who takes a womanist approach to black theology. A brief survey of their christologies will put us in a position to understand in more specific terms what it might mean for this subtradition to help form the Christs of the larger tradition.

In his early manifesto of the black theology movement, *Black Theology and Black Power*, published in 1969, Cone offers a shocking analysis of the social situation with which American christologies must be correlated: "On the American scene today, as yesterday, one problem stands out: the enslavement of black Americans."[2] It is doubtful that Cone would see things much differently today. After all, alongside the continuing growth of a black middle-class in this country, there is a well-nigh permanent black underclass, trapped in America's blighted inner cities. That latter community is ravaged day after day by drugs, violence, and the disintegration of its families. And the number of black persons caught in this underclass existence is all out of proportion to the total number of African Americans in our society.

It is to this American situation that Cone attempts to apply the gospel of Jesus as the Christ. He is convinced that the real Jesus Christ, as opposed to Christs that are ideological, self-serving projections of the privileged members of society, is precisely Christ the liberator of the poor and the oppressed. Cone's Christ is the one who begins his ministry by reading aloud in the synagogue from the prophet Isaiah, "The Spirit of the Lord is upon me, because he has anointed me to bring good news to the poor. He has sent me to proclaim release to the captives . . . to let the oppressed go free" (Luke 4:18).

For Cone, this is the historical Jesus, and it is crucial to keep our eyes fixed upon him if we are to avoid the creation of false Christs. Cone is quite aware, of course, that we have no easy access to the historical Jesus, and he certainly does not limit the reality of the Christ to the historical Jesus. He holds, for example, that "the Christian does not ask what Jesus would do, as if Jesus were confined to the first century. He asks: 'What is he doing? Where is he at work?'"[3] But there is, suggests Cone, a readily discernible "historical kernel" that must ever be kept in view:

> Taking seriously the New Testament Jesus, black theology believes that the historical kernel is the manifestation of Jesus as the Oppressed One whose earthly existence was bound up with the oppressed of the land. This is not to deny that other emphases are present. Rather it is to say that whatever is said about Jesus' conduct (Fuchs), about the manifestation of the expectant eschatological future in the deeds and words of Jesus (Bornkamm), or about his resurrection as the "ultimate confirmation of Jesus' claim to authority" (Pannenberg), it must serve to illuminate Jesus' sole reason for existence: to bind the wounds of the afflicted and to liberate those who are in prison.[4]

If we fail to keep the liberatory intent of the historical Jesus in view, then it is all-too-easy to mold our Christs to suit our ideologies. Thus, the "chief error of white American religious thought" is that it "allows the white condition to determine the meaning of Jesus. The historical Jesus must be taken seriously if we intend to avoid making Jesus into our own image."[5]

Cone wishes to keep the historical Jesus, attested to in the Bible, in dialectical relation with contemporary African American experience.[6] The Jesus of the Bible can only be the real Christ today if he speaks to the contemporary situation, but contemporary Christs of faith must, at the same time, always be responses to the real historical Jesus. The modern and contemporary African American experience, in particular, can productively be held in this kind of dialectical tension with the historical Jesus: the historical Jesus came to free the oppressed, and African Americans are the oppressed of this time and place.

It is clear, then, that while Cone is aware of the difficulties in finding the historical Jesus behind the biblical Christs of faith, he puts great emphasis upon what he takes to be the historical core of those biblical accounts. He is convinced that it confronts us with a Jesus whose purpose is to liberate the oppressed. His case is bolstered when we turn back to the criterion that Christ provides redemption. However tenuous the connection between the historical Jesus and living Christs of faith, the Christian community has always expected the latter to effect redemption. And while that redemption has often been conceived in ways that leave social, political, and economic oppression untouched, any such interpretation of redemption is hardly possible for us today. Today we understand the human person as, in significant measure, a creature of his or her place in a particular social setting. As we have already noted, human being is always "being-in-the-world," and any thoroughgoing account of what that means must go beyond Heidegger's own explicit reflections to a grasp of our concrete social and economic situatedness. Hence, if the Christ is to provide a redemption that touches our very being, he cannot neglect oppression, anymore than Cone's version of the historical Jesus neglected it. And in contemporary America, that means that the Christ must have something to say about the exploitation of African Americans.

Cone's theology suggests how the Christ offered redemption in the past, how he accomplishes it in the present, and how he will effect it in the future. We have already seen that the historical Jesus brought a message of liberation to the oppressed. He lived, taught, and healed among the outcasts of his world, those who had been forced to the margins of the social order. But the living Christ of faith redeems in the present too. It is by faith in Jesus Christ's constant identification with them that the oppressed are able to carry on in their struggles. The resurrected Christ in his role as the presence of God is all-important here:

> This vertical sense of personal relationship with the God of Jesus is log-
> ically prior to the other components of human liberation. For without
> the knowledge of God that comes through divine fellowship, the
> oppressed would not know that what the world says about them is a
> lie. They would have to believe what they are *made* to believe through
> police sticks and guns.[7]

This knowledge frees the Christian to attain the identity that God has
intended for him or her:

> freedom is *not doing what I will but becoming what I should. A man
> is free when he sees clearly the fulfillment of his being and is thus capa-
> ble of making the envisioned self a reality. . . .* Is this not why God
> became man in Jesus Christ so that man might become what he is? Is
> this not at least a part of what St. Paul had in mind when he said, "For
> freedom, Christ has set us free" (Gal. 5:1)?[8]

Thus, the vertical dimension, the presence of God through the Christ,
allows the oppressed to discern their real identities, in spite of the forces
that would impose lesser identities upon them. Furthermore, it empowers them to struggle in the historical or horizontal plane against those
same oppressive forces. Cone reminds us that "there is no true liberation
independent of the struggle for freedom in history," nor can one be liberated "without the commitment of revolutionary action against injustice, slavery, and oppression."[9]

With faith in the resurrection of the Christ as his starting point,
Cone can also affirm the future dimension of God's liberating activity.
This future dimension is not simply God's continuing presence within
human history, but also his eschatological work: "liberation is also
beyond history and not limited to the realities and limitations of this
world."[10] The resurrection of Christ represents the conquest of death.
But the Christian hope for life beyond this world need not become an
opiate in the Marxian sense. On the contrary, it is a hope that energizes
revolutionary struggle:

> If death is the ultimate power and life has no future beyond this world,
> then the rulers of the state who control the policemen and the military
> are indeed our masters. . . . But if the oppressed, while living in history,
> can nonetheless see beyond it, if they can visualize an eschatological
> future beyond the history of their humiliation, then "the *sigh* of the
> oppressed," to use Marx's phrase, can become a cry of revolution
> against the established order.[11]

It is just this revolutionary sigh, says Cone, that issues from the resurrection of Christ.

Cone is convinced, then, that the Christ provides the redemption
sought by oppressed persons, whether in first-century Palestine or in the

contemporary United States. It is Christ who makes God present to the oppressed so that they are assured of their dignity and value over against those who attempt to demean them. It is his example as the historical Jesus, his liberating activity in the present, and his eschatological future that empowers society's victims to courageously oppose the forces and structures of oppression. Furthermore, this Christ can liberate and redeem not only the oppressed, but the oppressors too. For example, he "makes possible the emancipation of blacks from self-hatred and frees whites from their racism."[12] And, as Cone points out, "to recognize that liberation is for oppressors because it is for all people prevents hate and revenge from destroying the revolutionary struggle."[13]

Cone's account of the sort of Christ that can bring redemption to the contemporary American scene receives an important qualification, if not corrective, in the work of various womanist theologians. These black women recognize that sexism is a powerful force for oppression. In this regard they agree with their white, feminist sisters. But black women's experience is still different from that of white women, for black women face the outrage not only of sexism, but also of racism and, oftentimes, classism. As a result, the white feminist movement does not address their needs for liberation. Thus, these black women define themselves not as "feminists," but as "womanists," a definition suggested by Alice Walker and based on an expression derived from the African American community:

> Womanist from womanish. (Opp. of "girlish," i.e., frivolous, irresponsible, not serious.) A Black feminist or feminist of color. From the Black folk expression of mothers to female children, "You acting womanish," i.e., like a woman. Usually referring to outrageous, audacious, courageous or willful behavior. Wanting to know more and in greater depth than is considered "good" for one. Interest in grown-up doings. Acting grown up. Being grown up. Interchangeable with another black folk expression: "You trying to be grown." Responsible. In charge. Serious.[14]

For a womanist theologian such as Jacquelyn Grant, then, "racism/sexism/classism, as a conglomerate representation of oppression, is the most adequate point of departure for doing . . . wholistic theology and Christology."[15] Unlike some feminist religious thinkers, womanist theologians recognize that sexism is not the sole form of oppression bedeviling contemporary society. And they know that "White women were just as much participants in . . . slavery as were White men."[16] Even after slavery was abolished, "White women were still oppressors and Black women were still the oppressed."[17] On the other hand, unlike the perspective afforded by Cone's early theology, womanist theologians recognize that combating racism alone is not sufficient if oppression is to be overcome.[18]

It might appear to some as if Grant's focus on black women's tri-dimensional experience of oppression—the experience of racism, sexism, and classism—so particularizes theology's concerns as to render it hopelessly parochial. But Grant argues that the opposite is the case. It is precisely in the experience of black women that the universal touches the particular.

> Black women share in the reality of a broader community. They share race suffering with Black men; with White women and other Third World women, they are victims of sexism; and with poor Blacks and Whites, and other Third World peoples, especially women, they are disproportionately poor.[19]

If the Christ frees the oppressed, and if the oppressed of our time and place are people of color in general, and black women in particular, then perhaps the most adequate picture of Christ is, as Grant suggests, the image of Christ as a black woman.[20]

This Christ claims to redeem the victims of racism, sexism, and classism. Redemption has usually been taken by the Christian tradition as the conquest of our estrangement from God. But how are we to understand the estrangement of black women and other oppressed persons? Certainly not as a result of their rebellion against God, but rather as their being cut off from God insofar as they are prevented from claiming their divine dignity as God's children. If rebellion against God is to figure into this account of estrangement and redemption, it will be found in the sinful behavior and structures that are part and parcel of racism, sexism, and classism.

What results when we confront the Christ (or Christs) of Cone and Grant with the reality of contemporary America, thinking particularly of the experience of African Americans in our inner cities? Does this Christ have any power, for instance, to redeem the crumbling social world described by Bell's statistics, in which an unconscionably large percentage of young black men is caught up in the criminal justice system? Let us be hard-nosed about our Christ-testing here. A realistic assessment of the situation must acknowledge, first of all, that to recognize those young men as victims of forces such as racism and classism is not to regard them all as wonderfully benign figures. Clearly, some of them are murderers, for example, that is, persons who have proved terribly destructive to themselves and others. On the other hand, because the number of black men who run afoul of the law in this country is so wildly out of proportion to the figures for the rest of the population, it is clear that we are confronting something much more complicated than a mere collection of individuals, each of whom has personally chosen to do wrong. Rather, it is apparent that young African American men in our country are disproportionately affected by destructive forces in the larger society.[21] Thus, while their behavior may be no less regrettable for ultimately having been caused by forces such as racism and poverty, it would appear to be explicable, in the final analysis, in terms of those evils, the very evils that are addressed by the Christ or Christs of black theology.

But just how successfully do the Christs of black theology actually address racism, sexism, and classism, and all of the phenomena that they bring in their wake, phenomena that seem to be devouring inner-city communities in our country? Can they provide redemption? This is an extraordinarily difficult question to answer, not least because of potential ambiguities with respect to what such a question even means. It is a question, then, that forces us to deal with a host of other, preliminary questions. For example, just what do we expect "redemption" to accomplish? Would genuine redemption simply eliminate the poverty and despair reflected in Bell's figures, or would it effect something more modest? And if the social crisis we are considering is rooted in the larger structure of contemporary American society, who has to embrace black theology's Christ or Christs in order for redemption of any sort to occur? Is it only young black men in America's inner cities who should embrace a black Christ, for instance, or is it equally necessary, or perhaps even more appropriate, for well-off white and black Americans to embrace black Christs?

Any attempt to adequately answer such questions would force us to confront basic issues within the larger Christian tradition. In other words, before we could answer questions about what redemption means in this particular context and about the redemptive efficacy of the Christs championed by Cone and Grant, we would need to explore the larger history of Christianity's claims for Christ's redemptive power, and we would need to think carefully about the varying degree of boldness in those diverse claims.[22] What, in the end, do Christians actually expect Christ as redeemer to do?

If we simply "look and see" what the Christs of black theology have accomplished thus far, it is easy to be pessimistic about their power. For one thing, black theology as a movement has not had the influence that its original proponents back in the 1960s envisioned for it. Thus, in a 1990 essay, Gayraud Wilmore observes,

> The failure of the new black theology, emerging from a coalition of academics, younger clergy, and ghetto revolutionaries, to penetrate the rank and file of the churches, is only one measure of the . . . sense of hopelessness, that descended upon black America as it entered the 1980s.

Today the almost complete breakdown of the family, the disorga-
nization of black labor constantly on the verge of economic catastro-
phe, the trivialization of black music, entertainment, and other forms
of our culture, and above all the losing battle against crack cocaine at
every level of our communities, are all signs of deculturation, demor-
alization, and the alienation of a confused black middle class from its
traditional role in the vanguard of the race. Under this baleful condition we see the church retreating into its stained glass foxholes.[23]

On the other hand, the failure of the churches to take up the kind
of black theology espoused by Cone and Grant does not necessarily
entail the impotence of the latter's versions of the Christ. Rather, it only
suggests that their Christs have not been embraced. As the title of
Wilmore's essay would have it, then, the project of black theology is "a
revolution unfulfilled, but not invalidated."

The most accurate assessment of the redemptive power of the
Christs of Cone and Grant is to say that we do not yet know whether
those Christs can contribute to the particular redemption that American
society now requires, the redemption of a social structure that has produced a demoralized and nearly permanent underclass. Certainly both
Cone and Grant would testify that their Christs have proved a source of
strength and meaning for the African American community in the past,
and that they are such a source for individual black persons in the present. But what impact these Christs can have on the larger dynamics of
American society is much harder to assess. What makes them uniquely
worthy of consideration, however, is that these particular imaginary
Christs have been self-consciously constructed with racism (and sexism
and classism) in view. In other words, while we cannot say exactly how
effective they might ultimately be in addressing the kind of American
tragedy represented by Bell's figures, these black Christs, unlike most
other Christs, confront such problems head-on. If that tragedy is to be
faced, if it is to be recognized as a genuine crisis that must be allowed to
help define the kind of redemption to be sought from a Christ in our
time and place, then the sorts of Christs set forth by Cone and Grant
must be given a chance to affect the Christ-formation of the larger
Christian tradition in America.

In addition to white churches, that larger American Christian tradition includes middle-class black Churches, Hispanic churches, and Asian
churches, to name the most obvious groups. But, for simplicity's sake, let
us concentrate here on the implications for those christologies that are,
for all practical purposes, white christologies.[24] How should the white
churches respond to the black Christs championed by Cone and Grant?

White Americans, as a group, seem particularly resistant at present
to the notion of corporate responsibility. While they appear to have lit-

tle difficulty with corporate pride—they can take pride in American success in the Gulf War or in the triumphs of various sports teams, even if
they as individuals made few if any contributions to these achievements—the majority of Americans do not feel in any way responsible for
social injustices. The regnant attitude seems to be that, if I do not personally mistreat the poor or harm another individual by a racist act, then
I am free of any connection with economic exploitation and racism. As
a result, it is more difficult at present to convince middle- and upper-
class American Christians that the plight of the disenfranchised should
affect the formation of their own versions of the Christ.

Thus, let us attempt to show the importance of black Christs to
white christologies, not by arguing in terms of *responsibility*, in the strict
sense, for unjust social conditions and practices, but rather by pointing
to what is at the very least a *connection* with those who suffer under the
unjust conditions and practices. First of all, white Americans and black
Americans, even those black Americans caught up in the implosion of
the inner cities, are members of the same society. While there are many
different points along the continuum of social privilege, those different
points are not wholly isolated from one another. On the contrary, the
various dynamics that form the numerous subgroups of American society are all interconnected. Thus, for example, the disappearance of fac-
tory jobs in the inner cities, which contributes in no small way to the
plight of inner-city black males, is part of the larger de-industrialization
of the American economy.

The connection of economically comfortable Christians with disadvantaged groups in our society is also apparent in the fact that notions
such as "privileged" and "disadvantaged" are by their very nature relative: the underclass is so defined precisely in relation to those who are
better off. "They" are the underclass just insofar as "we" are economically more secure than they are. This is not the same as saying that the
upper classes are responsible for the fact that other persons find themselves in an underclass existence, but it clearly suggests that we all exist
in inextricable connection to one another. Hence the ultimate inescapa-
bility of the biblical question, "Am I my brother's keeper?" (Genesis 4:9)
This question confronts us once again with the crisis character of the
challenge facing American society. The creation of a seemingly permanent underclass, the relegation of an incredible number of black men to
lives of despair and crime, and the general destruction of the social fab-
ric in huge sections of our cities, may well represent a crisis precisely in
the biblical sense: we are faced with a *krisis*, a judgment upon our
behavior, insofar as our response to this dilemma will determine our
corporate moral character.[25] How we answer the question about being
our brother's keeper will decide who we are as a people.

If all of this implies that the black Christs of the progressive sub-tradition represented by Cone and Grant ought to act back upon the larger community of American Christians to help form the latter's contemporary Christs of faith, just how should this influence be exercised? Suppose that we begin with a very general sort of influence: white American christologies today ought to acknowledge that Christ's work includes the task of liberating the oppressed. By way of analogy, consider the influence of Latin American theologies of liberation upon the larger christology of the Roman Catholic Church. In 1984, Cardinal Ratzinger, who is the head of the Vatican office responsible for maintaining theological orthodoxy in the Church, issued "An Instruction on Certain Aspects of the 'Theology of Liberation.'" While Ratzinger's principal concern may be to repudiate what the Vatican takes to be dangers in Latin American liberation theology, especially insofar as that theology imbibes elements of Marxism, the document also clearly reflects the impact of liberation thought upon the Church. It begins, for example, with the assertion that "the Gospel of Jesus Christ is a message of freedom and a force for liberation." Indeed, whatever criticisms the "Instruction" wishes to level at liberation theology, those criticisms "should not at all serve as an excuse for those who maintain an attitude of neutrality and indifference in the face of the tragic and pressing problems of human misery and injustice."[26] Perhaps white American Catholics and Protestants might respond to the black Christs of African American theology in a parallel fashion, and acknowledge that there is no ready excuse for ignoring the forces of racism, classism, and sexism in American society.

But what does this mean, more concretely, for how white American Christians imagine their Christs? Should they simply abandon their old images of the Christ and embrace something like Grant's Christ as a black woman? Whatever the wisdom of such a radical transformation, it is safe to say that it will not be an option considered by most white persons. White Christians will, for the most part, continue to imagine Christ as someone more like themselves, someone to whom they can more easily relate. Yet the reasonably sensitive among them will certainly be willing to acknowledge that their own Christs are incomplete, that there is more to Christ than one's own christological constructions can communicate. All Christs of faith, as imaginative attempts to grasp the presence of God in a tangible, human form, are limited.

But the mere recognition that all imaginary Christs are limited hardly seems sufficient here. The major difficulty is that this recognition seldom affects how one imagines the Christ; one goes on as before, with the admission of christological incompleteness as a mere afterthought. One says, in essence, "My Christ applies to my world, while other set-

tings may demand different images of Christ." But such compartmen-
talization of Christs, while it may be defensible in other cases, is inde-
fensible here: if I am a white *American* Christian, then the world
addressed by the black Christs of Cone and Grant is not a world entirely
separate from my own. I am unavoidably connected with that world,
and my Christ does not belong in a compartment separate from the
black Christs called forth by that world.

Thus, the black Christs championed by Cone and Grant ought to
have a real impact upon white Christs. And this means that, rather than
being merely a perfunctory afterthought, the recognition that white
Christs are limited, that they lack the redemptive power to address a
major American social crisis, must be integrated into the actual imaginative construction of white Christs. We must come to speak of a *constitutive incompleteness* in white Christs of faith. This expression may
appear to be an oxymoron: since the constitutive characteristics of something are what give it its identity, constitutive incompleteness seems to
suggest something whose identity is to have an incomplete identity. But
this is precisely the nature of a white Christ that has been formed in hon-
est confrontation with the black Christs described above. Such a white
Christ must, as part of its very identity, always call our attention to its
own need to be completed by other Christs. There must be a visible gap
in its being, a lack that paradoxically helps to define it.

Our discussion of the transcendence paradox in chapter 1 provided
an occasion to mention Paul Tillich's notion of the self-negating symbol
of the crucified Christ. The event of Christ on the cross, taken as an
image of the presence of God, focuses upon the negation that is cruci-
fixion, thereby highlighting the inadequacy of its own finite symbolic
content. As a result, it can more adequately point beyond itself to the
divine and ward off any idolatrous attachment to itself as a symbol.[27]
The referential dynamic involved in the symbol of the cross is vertical,
that is, from the finite symbolic material to the divine. But the referential dynamic that characterizes the constitutive incompleteness of the
white Christ is horizontal: it does not point away from itself and directly
to the divine, but away from itself toward other imaginary Christs, especially black Christs. It is only when it is held open to these other Christs,
and only when it works along with them, that it has, as a subsequent
moment, the chance to refer vertically to God as the power of redemption.

Let us make all of this more concrete by way of an example. Suppose that I am a financially secure white American and that the imaginary Christ that I embrace is one version of the "cosmic Christ." I
understand the Christ first and foremost as the Logos through whom all
things were created, the ordering and animating principle of the entire

cosmos. My devotional encounter with this Christ is through meditation upon the beauty and the power of the physical universe. Given our contemporary knowledge and sensibilities, this might well mean, for example, that I see the power of the Christ in Hubble telescope images of new stars coming to birth in distant galaxies, and that I believe ecological activism to be a concrete result of my Christian commitments.

When forced to contemplate the poverty and injustices suffered by a disproportionate number of persons of color in America, especially in our inner cities, I naturally turn to my image of the Christ. What does this Christ have to say to the crisis facing my society? Probably very little. But then my Christ fails as a redeemer. Either I must abandon this Christ altogether, or acknowledge its inadequacy in this regard and self-consciously embrace it as an incomplete Christ that must constantly be held open for completion by other Christs. This is a difficult task. I must somehow see to it that my thinking about the Christ is always accompanied by a recognition of the incompleteness of that thinking. Indeed, I must think incompleteness as a constitutive element of my Christ. But by what mechanism of thought can I accomplish this?

Perhaps this is possible only through the use of an image. For example, I might embrace the image of the cosmic Christ as the wounded Christ. Ordinarily I would confine the wounded Christ to the crucified Jesus of Nazareth, Jesus before his ascension.[28] And I would ordinarily think of the cosmic Christ as the Eternal Christ, the Christ who transcends the physical effects of the violence visited upon the earthly Jesus. But now I picture the cosmic Christ, the Christ who enlivens the entire universe, as unable to overcome the wounds inflicted by the cross. Those open wounds suggest the limitations, the constitutive incompleteness of the cosmic Christ; they hold this Christ open for other Christs of faith. The wounded cosmic Christ refers first to other Christs, and only subsequently, in concert with those other Christs, to the presence of God.

For my own Christ of faith to be held open for other Christs in this manner means that, in circumstances where my Christ is powerless to provide redemption, I must defer to those other Christs. When I recognize the inability of the cosmic Christ, at least according to our hypothetical example, to proffer redemption in the context of the crisis of social justice represented in Bell's figures, I also recognize that the cosmic Christ points away from himself to a black Christ. To the extent that I do not actually embrace a black Christ as my own, the incompleteness of my imaginary Christ is accompanied by an incompleteness in my piety: I have no object of religious devotion to which I can turn in this situation, but must be content in the knowledge that other persons are devoted to Christs that may have redemptive power in these circumstances.[29] There is another possibility here, however. The incompleteness of my own Christ might lead me to somehow adopt the other Christ or Christs to which my Christ points, to take them up in addition to my original Christ of faith. This is a possibility that we shall explore in greater detail in chapter 5.

Let us step back at this point and survey the landscape we have explored. Black theology represents an important subtradition of the larger Christian tradition, particularly the larger American Christian tradition. The black Christs set forth by thinkers such as James Cone and Jacquelyn Grant attempt to face head-on the injustices of racism, classism, and sexism as they prey upon American society. If white Christs are to be responsive to a society in crisis because of these injustices, then these white Christs will have to be informed in some way by black Christs. As a first step, the devotees of white Christs might simply acknowledge that, in addition to the Christ's other roles, he must be acknowledged to be the liberator of the oppressed. More significantly, white Christs must face their own incompleteness when confronted by black Christs. Little is accomplished by acknowledging this incompleteness only as an afterthought. One must fold the recognition of incompleteness into the very being of imaginary white Christs. Thus, we can speak of the constitutive incompleteness of white Christs of faith.

This is an example of a subtradition acting back in a powerful fashion upon the larger tradition.[30] It suggests one important way in which the many different Christs that exist within contemporary Christianity can interact with one another. And it puts us in a position to go on to think in some detail about what might result from self-conscious confrontation with the challenge of christological pluralism. When we engage in Christ-testing, where do we find ourselves at the end of the day? What are the possible results, in concrete terms, of such interpretive winnowing?

Before we can attempt to answer such questions, we must consider the "who" of this whole interpretive process. In other words, just who is going to make the interpretive judgments via which imaginary Christs are sorted out? It turns out that there are several different levels at which this interpretive work can go on. On the most basic level, the individual Christian may well engage in the process of Christ-testing. If he or she is to embrace a particular Christ and pass by others thoughtfully rather than arbitrarily, then at least a rudimentary kind of interpretive sorting will be required. Perhaps those first-century persons who were confronted directly by the historical Jesus were spared the responsibility of Christ-testing. Indeed, the New Testament accounts of such encounters suggest that Jesus' call to discipleship could result in an immediate, uncalculating response on the part of those at whom it was directed; Jesus' words tested his hearers, rather than his hearers testing Jesus and his message.[31] But later Christians find themselves in a quite different situation. They are confronted not by the historical individual Jesus of Nazareth, but by a host of competing interpretations or versions of Jesus as the Christ. This is true even for one who relies entirely on the New Testament and ignores later imaginary Christs, for the New Testament already presents us with numerous Christs. Thus, one must always decide which of the many Christs that beckon should in fact really be followed. Christ-testing becomes an unavoidable task and responsibility.

But Christ-testing is not the responsibility simply of the individual Christian. Most Christians are members of a larger community of faith, a particular congregation and probably a denomination with which that congregation is associated. Thus, the individual's Christ-testing is part of the Christ-testing of these larger communities. Whether the average individual's own interpretive decisions have a significant impact on this larger discussion, or whether real interpretive authority tends to reside with theologians and church officials, depends of course on the particular circumstances. In any case, strategies for rejecting some Christs as illegitimate as well as strategies for recognizing complementary Christs will be important both on the level of the individual believer and on the community level. The individual must be able to reject some Christs in order to decide which particular Christ to embrace. And he or she may also need interpretive strategies that allow for an awareness of complementarity among Christs, as in the case of the constitutive incompleteness of white American Christs. As for a community of faith, such as a congregation or subtradition, it too must be able to reject some Christs, in order to maintain a particular identity. At the same time, it must have strategies that can recognize genuinely complementary Christs, so as to make sense of the inevitable christological pluralism in its midst. Given the results of our investigation thus far, what specific strategies are available?

One can begin the sorting process by rejecting some Christs. If the criteria that we have considered above have any teeth, then it must certainly be possible to simply put some Christs aside as inadequate. For instance, if one decides, as Reinhold Niebuhr apparently did, that the Christ prescribed by Norman Vincent Peale as a balm for our ills fails to provide any genuine redemption, then one will disregard Peale's Christ. That Christ will simply be left behind in the ongoing pluralistic christological conversation. While different interpreters may well decide the issue differently, the principle still obtains: those Christs that appear neither to exemplify nor to adequately address criteria such as those outlined earlier—Christs should bear a clear family resemblance to the Christs of the New Testament, they must make God present, and they ought to provide redemption—will be allowed to fall from view.

Of course, we should not underplay the fact that different interpreters will perhaps make different decisions about which Christs fail to address the criteria adequately. On the one hand, the ability to reject some imaginary Christs on the basis of criteria such as those we have discussed above is an important opening move in the effort to confront the potential chaos of christological manyness. It allows us at least to orient ourselves in the larger christological discussion. On the other hand, there is a sense in which christological pluralism outruns any attempts to master it. My community will attempt to bring a degree of order to the scene by rejecting some christological claimants. Your community will make the same attempt, but may come to different decisions about which Christs fail to pass muster. Thus, this first strategy for facing the pluralism of Christs is itself pluralistic. In addition, different communities may not even be able to agree upon the criteria that should be used for Christ-testing. Yet the very fact that it is possible to have a conversation about which criteria to adopt for Christ-testing, and about the results of applying particular criteria, still provides a starting point for addressing the confusing array of imaginary Christs.

Let us move, then, to a second strategy for confronting christological pluralism. *It is possible to determine that some Christs are different from, but also <u>clearly</u> <u>complementary</u> to, one's own imaginary Christ.* Thus, in chapter 3 we noted the possibility that my own Christ of faith might focus on the salvation of the individual human being, but that this Christ could be understood as consistent with a Christ who liberates the oppressed from unjust social structures. In other words, my own religious center of gravity is in the first Christ, but I acknowledge the validity of the second and am open to having my concept of the Christ expanded by this other Christ.[32] This interpretive stance is given particular salience by the phenomenon of constitutive incompleteness that we have just seen in our juxtaposition of white Christs with the black Christs championed by Cone and Grant. If our own Christ is constitutively incomplete, then we will not only acknowledge that other Christs can exist side-by-side with our own without contradicting our own Christ, but we will have to self-consciously open our Christ to one or more of those others as a *necessary* complement. The redemptive incompleteness of white American Christs, for example, demands that those Christs refer to black Christs before they can refer to the presence of God.

If the first interpretive strategy for meeting the challenge of christological pluralism—employing criteria that allow us to reject some Christs—holds out the possibility of decreasing the number of christological claimants, this second strategy—recognizing that some other Christs are clearly complementary to our own—already makes it clear that we are not headed for a narrow christological exclusivism. On the contrary, the goal of our interpretive sorting should be a productive conversation among a pluralism of Christs. The remaining strategies only serve to enhance that genuinely pluralistic conversation.

The third of these strategies is to *allow for <u>possible complementarity</u> where the relationship between different Christs is ambiguous*. This takes us into the realm of analogy and symbol, inasmuch as the use of analogy and symbol in the construction of imaginary Christs is often what makes the potential complementarity of different Christs uncertain. Let us take the issue in several steps, beginning with the use of analogy and symbol in talking about God. In the terminology I shall use here, the statement "God is good" is analogical. The word "good" is an abstract term, derived from our knowledge of human behavior, that we apply to God by way of analogy. That is, though the use of the word overlaps in the two cases of human behavior and divine behavior, it does not mean exactly the same thing in those two cases; the divine goodness is perfect, far transcending the good of which human beings are capable. Yet, while it is only human goodness of which we have firm knowledge, the word "good" applies most literally, because perfectly, to God.

The statement "God is a mother" can be interpreted as symbolic. The word "mother," like the term "good," is taken from our experience of human beings. But whereas the abstract analogical term "good" applies literally to God, the symbolic term "mother" applies only nonliterally to God. In both cases, however, the analogical and the symbolic, our everyday use of the words is being imaginatively stretched in order to refer to something beyond the world of our ordinary experience.

If analogies and symbols are used to talk about God, then they will also be used to talk about the presence of God in the Christ. Thus, Christians will make analogical statements such as "Christ is just," or "Christ forgives sins." We know what human justice is like, and we know what it means for human beings to forgive one another. But we do not fully grasp what it means for God in Christ to be just or to forgive sins. We only know that Christ is perfectly just and offers perfect forgiveness. If, to take but one example, my deliberations as to whether to forgive someone involve a calculation of how much the person to be forgiven has hurt me, this is due to a weakness in my character that does not apply to the perfect forgiveness offered by God in Christ. Yet, while I can say that Christ's forgiveness is free of imperfection, I cannot grasp exactly what his perfect forgiveness is like. But this element of ignorance that accompanies the use of analogy points to the notion of *possible* complementarity between different Christs. Suppose that your Christ is focused on bringing justice to the world and mine is focused upon the forgiveness of sins. Let us assume, furthermore, that it is not immediately apparent that these two approaches to the Christ can be reconciled. The fact remains that we cannot say for sure that they are irreconcilable, for neither of us has a firm grasp on just what christic justice or christic forgiveness entails. Thus, while the second strategy involved holding in conversation different Christs that were *clearly* complementary, this third strategy involves recognizing that different Christs *may* be complementary even when we cannot grasp that complementarity.

This possibility is equally clear in the case of what I am calling symbolic statements about the Christ. Consider the two symbolic assertions "Christ is the Good Shepherd" and "Christ is the Lamb of God." On the surface, these two images cannot be reconciled: Christ cannot be both the shepherd and one of the sheep. But, of course, the fact that they would clash if taken literally says nothing about their compatibility as symbols or metaphors. There are many instances in which I can use quite different metaphorical images to describe the same reality. Indeed, it is not difficult in this particular case to regard the images as ultimately complementary. But consider the fact that good symbols often hold more meaning than I am able immediately to grasp. For one thing, they resonate not only on the conscious but also on the unconscious level. Furthermore, they are always open to new interpretations in the future. Suppose, then, that we juxtapose two imaginary Christs and that each is constituted, in part, by a symbol or symbols.[33] Let us, assume, furthermore, that, at least initially, these two Christs appear to be in tension with one another rather than to complement one another. Despite this apparent incompatibility, the fact that I cannot immediately grasp the full import of the symbols that make up these two Christs suggests that I cannot immediately be certain that they are in fact incompatible. Must I not take seriously the possibility that they are ultimately complementary?

A fourth scenario that deserves consideration is one that we briefly considered already in chapter 3: at least where providential Christs are concerned, *we may encounter a situation in which two Christs definitely contradict one another—they cannot be regarded as complementary—but it is impossible to determine which Christ, if either, is genuine.* Our specific example in chapter 3 involved not two full-blown imaginary Christs in opposition to one another, but two different ethical injunctions that might result from two different Christs. Suppose that one Christ counsels pacifism in the face of something like Nazism and Hitler's march across Europe, while a second counsels armed resistance. If we embrace providential Christs, believing in a God who is a personal consciousness who self-consciously reveals Godself in the person of the Christ, then it is reasonable to assume that one of these courses of behavior is probably more consistent with God's intention in the Christ than the other. But it is certainly possible that we will end up having to admit that there is no convincing way to demonstrate that one of them is in fact the right course of action. At the end of the day, you may still prefer the pacifist Christ and I the more aggressive Christ, given our own larger sensibilities, but we will each admit that the issue is undecidable purely in terms of argumentative application of christological criteria. As a result, two contradictory ethical stances, and perhaps two clearly contradictory Christs, may be allowed to stand side-by-side within the same community of faith.

We encounter a variation on this fourth theme when we consider nonprovidential Christs. Recall that, in that case, *it is possible to decide that two genuinely contradictory Christs must both be accepted as perfectly valid.* Again, one Christ may command a pacifist response to injustice and aggression, another armed resistance. And perhaps neither can be rejected on the basis of the criteria that we have proposed for Christ-testing. These two Christs cannot be reconciled. But because in this case we are thinking of God as a reality without personal consciousness, it makes no sense to say that in the inner mind of God one of these ethical avenues is the right one and the other wrong. Thus, we are left with the conclusion, not that it is impossible to determine which of these two contradictory Christs is valid, but that they are both valid even though genuinely contradictory.

All of these strategies for dealing with christological pluralism are potentially productive. The first strategy brings some order to the scene by reducing the number of christological candidates. All of the other strategies result in an individual or community acknowledging a plurality of Christs as valid. But this too brings order out of chaos. Rather than constituting mere resignation in the face of an overwhelming pluralism, these other strategies reveal a purposeful pattern of interrelationships among the plethora of Christs. That is, we come to understand which other Christs are complementary with our own and just why they are complementary. Instead of a chaotic multiplicity, we now have a meaningful pluralism within which it is possible to orient ourselves.

But important questions remain. What precisely is involved in recognizing that other Christs complement one's own? How far can one go toward embracing those other Christs, or at least allowing them to reconfigure one's own imaginary Christ? Must we now think in terms of a new kind of christological consciousness? While I shall make no pretense of being able to answer such questions, it will be the task of the next chapter to articulate them in more detail.

CHAPTER 5

My Christ, Other Christs, and the Buddha: Toward a New Christological Consciousness?

Fundamental questions are posed by the prospect of affirming one's own Christ while opening that Christ, and oneself, to other imaginary Christs. These questions have to do with the very nature of Christian devotion. We shall consider several such questions in turn, proposing not to answer them, but to explore their ramifications.

First, *can one actually appropriate other Christs?* We have seen that it is possible to recognize other Christs as complementary to one's own. This should entail, as a minimum, that one feels comfortable as part of a community in which others devote themselves to these different Christs. More seems to be demanded if one finds oneself having to think one's own Christ as constitutively incomplete. Then it is not enough to simply accept, or even celebrate, the fact that other persons worshipping beside one embrace different versions of the Christ. Rather, it then becomes necessary to admit that one's own Christ cannot function effectively as a self-contained entity, but refers beyond itself to another Christ, as when the constitutively incomplete Christs of white American piety refer to black Christs. The least that is demanded here is that one defer in certain circumstances to those other Christs, recognizing that one's own Christ does not have the redemptive efficacy required in that setting. This means, in effect, deferring to the other persons who embrace the potentially more efficacious Christ or Christs. Hence, there is a lacuna in one's own piety at this point.

But what about taking another step? Might it be possible for me not just to defer to those other Christs, but to actually embrace them, incorporating them into my own religious consciousness and practice? Can one, in other words, devote oneself to a multiplicity of fully formed imaginary Christs? In such a case, I would not just acknowledge that other Christs complement mine and thus belong alongside my own in the sense that they should be embraced by other members of my church. Nor would I simply borrow some attractive elements from those other Christs and tack them onto my own imaginatively construed Christ, as when I allow that Christ, whom I picture as focused upon the salvation of the individual, is also concerned to free the oppressed. Instead, I would have to actually affirm more than one Christ, in a way that substantively informed my worldview and behavior, even if each Christ were imaginatively well rounded and thus individuated. In some situations I would turn to one Christ, in other situations to other Christs; one image of Christ would be at the center of some of my devotional practices, and other Christs at the center of other practices.

Perhaps this is where constitutive incompleteness ultimately leads. For example, I picture the cosmic Christ as wounded, as being held open to black Christs. But this finally means not just deferring to those black Christs, or deferring to other persons who embrace such Christs, but actually embracing a black Christ or Christs myself. And why should I stop with just two Christs? Might it not be desirable to commit myself to three Christs, or to five?

If the attempt actually to embrace a multitude of Christs is to succeed, there must be some way to hold onto a sense of unity in the midst of diversity. On the one hand, there may be a benefit in embracing Christs that stand in some degree of tension with one another. Perhaps that will stretch my religious sensibilities. But, on the other hand, if the various Christs that I have embraced simply contradict one another, the result will be existential and ethical paralysis. Where might we find the requisite unity amidst diversity, then?

One possibility would be to see that unity as a function of the Christian community of which I am a part.[1] Let us assume that the various Christs to whom I devote myself have all been made known to me initially through the piety of other members of my church community. In a strong ecclesiology, such as the kind embraced by most Roman Catholic thinkers, for example, the church is the body of Christ. It is the fundamental fashion in which Christ is tangible for us, the continuing presence of the eternal Christ within time.[2] From the vantage point of this kind of strong ecclesiology, the different imaginary Christs that I embrace can be held together by the fact that they are all rooted in and help to inform the life of the church in which I participate. They have a concrete, pragmatic unity, insofar as they are all manifestations of the one Christ whose body is the Christian community and who is realized in that unified community.

One variation on this approach is suggested by Rosemary Radford

Ruether's version of spirit christology, which was mentioned in chapter 3. Ruether holds that the Christ can be present to us today in the form of our sisters and brothers; I see the Christ in the way of being of various members of the Christian community. To the extent that the particular Christs that I embrace are manifested in other persons, and inasmuch as I participate with these others in a single community, then the various Christs to which I devote myself are pragmatically unified in the life of that community.

As a second option, one might hold that it is possible to embrace a number of imaginary Christs simultaneously because those different Christs are unified by one's concept of God "above" them and the figure of Jesus of Nazareth "below" them. That is, I hold, first of all, to a particular notion of the divine. All of the imaginary Christs that I embrace will be understood as manifestations of this one God and will be tested for consistency with this God (though they may also act back on my understanding of God). To employ the Hindu vocabulary once more, all of my imaginary Christs fit together insofar as they are all simply different avatars of the one Godhead.[3] Furthermore, I regard each of the imaginary Christs that I embrace as a legitimate response to the historical man, Jesus of Nazareth. While it will be true that I have no direct access to the historical Jesus, something like consistency with the Christs of the New Testament might be taken as at least suggesting proximity to the historical Jesus on the part of all of my Christs.

A third possible avenue to unity would be to self-consciously focus upon one particular imaginary Christ as one's guiding Christ-image. One could embrace other imaginary Christs as long as they did not contradict that guiding version of the Christ. This would not rule out the possibility of devoting oneself to other Christs that are in some kind of productive tension with one's central Christ; it would only disallow Christs that are thoroughly incompatible with that christological center of gravity.

Would any of these proposed sources of unity work in actual practice, so that one could really develop an internally pluralistic christological consciousness, embracing a multitude of different, fully realized Christs? This question probably cannot be answered at the present moment in Christian history. But the pluralistic exigencies of the contemporary scene suggest that these strategies will be tested out in Christian experience in the not-too-distant future.

That same pluralistic scene confronts us with another important query: *Can a Christian today embrace another redeemer figure (or other redeemer figures) in addition to the Christ?* If we can contemplate a consciousness constituted by devotion to a multitude of Christs, why not a consciousness that embraces both the Christ and the Buddha, or the Christ and Krishna, for example? This second question has actually been explored in more detail by Christian thinkers than the question about devoting oneself to a number of different Christs. After all, the pluralistic world in which we exist today has already produced a phenomenon sometimes referred to with the expression "multiple religious identities": there are already persons who think of themselves as both Christian and Buddhist, or Hindu and Christian, for instance.

Suppose that we briefly consider the question, "Can one devote oneself to both the Christ and the Buddha?" This is not the place, nor do I have the expertise on Buddhism and its relation to Christianity, actually to answer this question. I pose it here simply as an example via which it is possible to note some of the implications of devotion to more than one redeemer figure. What follows, then, is intended as merely a brief overview of the issues involved and an indication of avenues that would need to be explored if one were seriously to investigate the relation of the Buddha to the Christ.[4]

The possibility of devoting oneself to both the Christ and the Buddha does not seem too farfetched if we focus simply upon the teaching of the two figures, and understand their teaching as consisting of relatively self-contained spiritual dicta, unencumbered by larger doctrinal or worldview considerations. It has often been observed, for instance, that the Sermon on the Mount and the *Dhammapada* appear to contain much parallel advice. Thus, Roy Amore can aver that "in spite of their different cultural backgrounds, Gautama and Jesus gave their disciples remarkably similar instructions for the development of a pure mind."[5] He goes on to argue that both masters counsel their followers to overcome anger, to avoid lust, not to be judgmental, to be content with whatever comes to them, and to store up heavenly treasures.

Things undoubtedly become more complicated if we approach the Christ and the Buddha, as perhaps we must, as imaginary Christs and imaginary Buddhas ensconced in particular philosophical and doctrinal contexts. Hence, when John Cobb asks the question, "Can a Christian be a Buddhist, too?" he feels it necessary to confront specific issues such as these: "Can a Christian accept as a goal the dissolution of personal existence? Can a Christian appropriate the vision of ultimate reality as Emptiness? Can a Christian enter fully into the sheer immanence in the moment that is required for Enlightenment?"[6] Cobb goes on to express his "conviction that not only will it be possible for a Christian to be a Buddhist, too, but that both thinking through and acting out this possibility are increasingly urgent claims upon us. Christianity needs Buddhism."[7] Such a view is possible, of course, only on the basis of certain other views about the nature of the Christian tradition: "We have many norms and convictions, but we erect none of them into the timeless essence of Christianity."[8]

Some persons do perhaps, in actual practice, live out this kind of multiple religious identity. Thus, the well-known Vietnamese Buddhist monk and spiritual leader, Thich Nhat Hanh explains that "on the altar of my hermitage in France, I have statues of Buddhas and bodhisattvas and also an image of Jesus Christ. I do not feel any conflict within me. Instead I feel stronger because I have more than one root."[9] Of course, the two roots are not of equal importance. The Buddhist root nourishes Thich Nhat Hanh more thoroughly than does the Christian one. Drawing upon Cobb's vocabulary, we might say that Hahn is a Buddhist and a Christian, too.

In any case, if this kind of question—can one embrace both the Christ and the Buddha?—has already frequently been asked in contemporary Christian thought, and if we are to make no pretense of really answering it, why even bother to restate it here? It is worth restating because it is being posed now from a particular, and perhaps new, vantage point. Rather than arising just as a function of the general religious pluralism of our day, the question arises here out of the internal dynamics of Christian consciousness. That is, the historically unique christological pluralism of our own time suggests the possibility of a Christian consciousness in which one embraces a host of different Christs. And this, in turn, leads to the question of whether it might not be possible to construct a genuine multiple religious identity, in which one can look not only to a Christ or Christs, but also to a Buddha or Buddhas. Of course, just to the extent that we have begun with a particular christological consciousness, our approach to the possibility of a multiple religious identity is a decidedly Christian one. In other words, the Christian tradition is our primary vantage point from which to view both Christs and Buddhas. We are asking, with Cobb, whether one who is first and foremost a Christian can be a Buddhist, too.

Thus, in this kind of approach to multiple religious identity, one stands within one particular religious tradition, and draws upon other traditions from the vantage point of that first, native tradition. One may be able to speak, as Thich Nhat Hanh does, of having two roots, but the second root must be, for all practical purpose, grafted onto the first as a secondary source of spiritual nourishment. To change metaphors, we are situated within the Christian tradition, and we attempt to translate elements of the Buddhist tradition into the Christian idiom. The two traditions are not wholly incommensurable. Christians are attracted to the figure of the Buddha only because there are significant points of contact between the contents of the two traditions. But the appropriation of

Buddhist elements will always be a translation, rather than some kind of immediate apprehension.

This leads to our third, and final, question: *Can one stand outside both the Christian and the Buddhist traditions (for example) and appropriate the Christ and the Buddha via those traditions?* There seems to be a significant number of persons today who do not directly identify with any of the great religious traditions of the world, yet wish to devote themselves in some fashion to figures such as Jesus Christ and the Buddha. In chapter 2, I argued that Christs need to be rooted in the Christian tradition if they are to have a genuinely objective identity. That my Christ has its roots in the Christian tradition, and has been tested by it, is what guarantees that when I refer to the "Christ," I am referring to essentially the same reality as intended by persons in the past when they spoke of "Christ." Thus, it would appear initially that one cannot in fact stand outside the Christian and Buddhist traditions and appropriate the Christ and the Buddha, at least not if one wishes to avoid the problem of mere subjective projection where one's Christs and Buddhas are concerned. But notice that I have posed the question this way: "Can one stand outside both the Christian and the Buddhist traditions and appropriate the Christ and the Buddha *via those traditions*?" In other words, the question is asking about the possibility of somehow respecting the objective rooting of the Christ and the Buddha in their respective traditions even though one stands outside them.

As always, it is helpful to think in terms of a concrete example: Suppose that I do not identify with any particular religious tradition. Yet I wish to construct a religious way of existence around the Christ and the Buddha. Instead of going the route of a New Age enthusiast, reconstructing the Christ and the Buddha however I see fit and without any compunctions about their objective integrity, I attempt to respect the origins of these figures in their traditions. Thus, rather than beginning with only the barest notions of the Christ and the Buddha and then idiosyncratically reconfiguring them, I start with the New Testament and the Fathers, and with traditional Therevada and Mahayana texts. Only after having seriously encountered the two redeemers in these sources do I attempt to fold the Buddha and the Christ into my own unique spirituality.

This approach is not without serious potential difficulties. First of all, while the texts upon which I might very conscientiously draw may suffice to put me in touch with the heritage of the two traditions, they will not introduce me to the *living* Christian tradition or the *living* Buddhist tradition. Thus, though my Christ and my Buddha may begin as the objective Christ and the objective Buddha of their respective traditions, once I begin to reconfigure them they will follow a different trajectory. While the Christ and the Buddha are constantly being reconstructed within their own traditions, my reconstruction will necessarily move them in directions that they would not move if the reworking were taking place in the larger context of the contemporary Christian and Buddhist traditions.

Of course, from some vantage points all of this may be perfectly acceptable. One might argue that one has avoided mere subjective projection, since one has started with tradition-generated pictures of the Buddha and the Christ. It is no weakness that, because one stands outside the two traditions, one's Buddha and Christ subsequently move off in a unique direction. On the contrary, this is merely to develop other potentials genuinely latent within the figures of the Christ and the Buddha, potentials that will unfortunately remain untapped within the two religious traditions.

But more needs to be said about the potential problems with appropriating Christs and Buddhas from a traditionless perspective. Even if we grant that it is desirable to have imaginary Christs and Buddhas that follow trajectories different from those generated by their traditions—and by no means all of their devotees will in fact grant this—there is still the issue of relying on an overly individualistic mechanism of Christ- and Buddha-formation. In other words, quite apart from the fact that I am not rooted in either the specifically Christian tradition or the specifically Buddhist tradition in this scenario, the further fact of the matter is that I am not rooted in any community at all: my imaginative construction of the Christ and the Buddha will be an essentially solitary undertaking. It takes place without the benefit of some larger religious or spiritual group in which I participate. As a result, the danger of subjective projection is still with us at this point. There will be nothing akin to Ruether's christic sisters and brothers to check the more idiosyncratic and potentially self-serving impulses of my imaginative constructions.

Even this objection does not constitute a definitive refutation of the possibility of appropriating the Christ and the Buddha outside of a religious tradition, of course. A proponent of that possibility might well point out, for example, that groups of persons, including the communities that constitute religious traditions, have sometimes proved more destructive than even relatively self-absorbed individuals. The Crusades and the Inquisition and ethnic cleansing in Bosnia and Kosovo all come to mind as examples.

I have attempted to unpack the implications of three questions suggested by the phenomenon of christological pluralism: Can one actually appropriate other Christs? Can a Christian today embrace another redeemer figure (or other redeemer figures) in addition to the Christ? Might it be possible to stand outside both the Christian and Buddhist traditions and appropriate the Christ and the Buddha (for example) via those traditions? Each of these questions brings others in its wake. I have refrained from drawing any firm conclusions about these matters. They are issues that are presently being explored on what can only be regarded as the frontiers of our expanding christological consciousness. That they will be decided by concrete religious practice at some point in the near future makes that future a religiously exciting prospect.

NOTES

CHAPTER ONE. HISTORICAL JESUSES AND IMAGINARY CHRISTS

1. See John Macquarrie's treatment of these titles in *Jesus Christ in Modern Thought* (Philadelphia: Trinity Press International, 1990), pp. 35–47. And note Gregory J. Riley's point that there were many models in the ancient world for classifying beings, and in their attempt to figure out who Jesus was, "the various churches and theologians seem, at one time or another, to have tried them all." See *One Jesus, Many Christs: How Jesus Inspired Not One True Christianity, But Many; The Truth about Christian Origins* (San Francisco: HarperCollins, 1997), p. 127.

2. This plurality of images of Jesus Christ is well documented in Jaroslav Pelikan's *Jesus Through the Centuries: His Place in the History of Culture* (New Haven: Yale University Press, 1985). Note however that, as the book's subtitle suggests, Pelikan ranges beyond the confines of Christian piety to the place of Jesus in the larger history of Western culture.

3. The classic article on the subject is Robert Bellah, "Civil Religion in America," *Daedalus* 96 (Winter 1967): 1–21.

4. Bruce Barton, *The Man Nobody Knows: A Discovery of the Real Jesus* (Indianapolis: Bobbs-Merrill, 1925).

5. Norman Vincent Peale, *The Power of Positive Thinking* (New York: Fawcett Crest, 1963; first published 1952).

6. Mark L. Prophet and Elizabeth Clare Prophet, *The Lost Teachings of Jesus*, 4 vols. (Livingston, Mont.: Summit University Press, 1986).

7. *Edgar Cayce's Story of Jesus*, edited by Jeffrey Furst (New York: Berkley, 1976).

8. See, for example, *The Gnostic Scriptures: Ancient Wisdom for the New Age*, translated with annotations and introductions by Bentley Layton, The Anchor Bible Reference Library (New York: Doubleday, 1987). This is a scholarly resource with a subtitle and cover art that seem intended to appeal to devotees of New Age spirituality.

9. See Pelikan, *Jesus Through the Centuries*, Chapter 10.

10. See ibid., chapter 5.

11. This is apparently part of the appeal of Matthew Fox's *The Coming of the Cosmic Christ: The Healing of Mother Earth and the Birth of a Global Renaissance* (San Francisco: Harper & Row, 1988).

12. Stephen Mitchell, *The Gospel According to Jesus: A New Translation and Guide to His Essential Teachings for Believers and Unbelievers* (New York: HarperCollins, 1991).

13. As translated in the New Revised Standard Version (NRSV), the passage reads, "For God so loved the world that he gave his only Son, so that everyone who believes in him may not perish but may have eternal life." All subsequent biblical quotations are also from the NRSV, National Council of the Churches of Christ, 1989.

14. My discussion of the history of the quest follows W. Barnes Tatum, *In Quest of Jesus: A Guidebook* (Atlanta: John Knox Press, 1982), chapter 5.

15. Ibid., p. 70.

16. See Albert Schweitzer, *The Quest of the Historical Jesus*, translated by W. Montgomery (New York: Macmillan, 1968).

17. The initial stirrings of a new interest in the historical Jesus were the result of Ernest Käsemann's work in the 1950s. Some of the most important current works are Marcus J. Borg, *Jesus: A New Vision* (San Francisco: Harper & Row, 1987) and *Jesus in Contemporary Scholarship* (Valley Forge, Pa.: Trinity Press International, 1994); Raymond E. Brown, *The Death of the Messiah: From Gethsemane to the Grave: A Commentary on the Passion Narratives in the Four Gospels* (New York: Doubleday, 1994); John Dominic Crossan, *The Historical Jesus: The Life of a Mediterranean Jewish Peasant* (San Francisco: HarperCollins, 1991).

18. See Marcus Borg, *Jesus in Contemporary Scholarship*, chapter 9.

19. See note 17 above.

20. John Dominic Crossan, *The Historical Jesus*, p. xxvii. Crossan also refers to Daniel J. Harrington's presidential address to the Catholic Biblical Association in 1986 in which Harrington listed seven different images of Jesus currently set forth by New Testament scholars: Jesus as (1) political revolutionary, (2) magician, (3) Galilean charismatic, (4) Galilean rabbi, (5) Hillelite or proto-Pharisee, (6) Essene, and (7) eschatological prophet. See ibid.

21. See the epilogue in ibid.

22. Paul Tillich, foreword in Martin Kähler, *The So-Called Historical Jesus and the Historic Biblical Christ*, translated, edited, and with an introduction by Carl E. Braaten (Philadelphia: Fortress, 1964), p. x.

23. Quoted by Braaten in his introduction to ibid., p. 10.

24. See Paul Tillich, *Systematic Theology*, 3 vols. (Chicago: University of Chicago, 1951–63), 2:102–38. Kähler already speaks of the "*Bild*" of Jesus. See *The So-Called Historical Jesus and the Historic Biblical Christ*, p. 47n.3.

25. See Edward Schillebeeckx, *Jesus: An Experiment in Christology*, translated by Hubert Hoskins (New York: Crossroad, 1979).

26. See, e.g., Karl Rahner, *Foundations of Christian Faith: An Introduction to the Idea of Christianity*, translated by William V. Dych (New York: Seabury, 1978). Rahner by no means denies the relevance of the historical Jesus altogether. For a discussion of the extent to which Christian faith must be grounded in the actual historical figure of Jesus, see pp. 236–54.

27. *Catechism of the Catholic Church* (New Hope, Ky.: Urbi et Orbi, 1994), p. 208 (paragraph 788). The material quoted by the *Catechism* is from Vatican II's *Lumen gentium*.

28. It is equally true that different philosophers will conceive this imaginative and constructive element differently. Kant, the father of the modern philo-

sophical disposition to see a creative role for the mind in its approach to reality, understands the constructive activity of the mind as a function of universal and invariant structures of subjectivity, while later hermeneutical theory puts more emphasis upon the unique interpretive activities of particular traditions, groups, and individuals.

29. By scientific data collection, I mean the individual acts of acquiring data, not the creation of the larger theoretical frameworks within which all data collection takes place. The latter obviously involves a larger amount of imaginative construction, a fact often highlighted in contemporary philosophies of science. It seems evident, however, that even the scientific enterprise taken as a whole is less dependent upon the imagination than are Christs of faith, since Christs of faith are focused on something that transcends the physical universe. Those doctrinaire postmodernists intent upon overturning every vestige of the Enlightenment tend to extend the range of constructive imagination indiscriminately and to exaggerate its role in the natural sciences. The special role of imagination in religious consciousness has been extensively explored and has been approached from a variety of perspectives. As a sample, see James P. Mackey, ed. *Religious Imagination* (Edinburgh: Edinburgh University Press, 1986); Gordon D. Kaufman, *The Theological Imagination: Constructing the Concept of God* (Philadelphia: Westminster, 1981); Michael L. Raposa, *Boredom and the Religious Imagination* (Charlottesville: University Press of Virginia, 1999).

30. Quoted in H. Richard Niebuhr, *Christ and Culture* (New York: Harper & Row, 1951), p. 77.

31. See John Macquarrie's treatment of Kierkegaard on the absolute paradox, in *Jesus Christ in Modern Thought*, p. 239.

32. For example, Kierkegaard asks us to imagine a poor man who is sent for by the emperor and told that the emperor wants him, an insignificant day-laborer, to be the emperor's son-in-law. How could the poor man bring himself to believe such an apparently absurd notion? But how much harder, suggests Kierkegaard, is the movement of faith, which entails accepting the idea that the infinite God deigns to enter into relation to me in the person of the Christ. The parable is from *The Sickness Unto Death*. It is reproduced in *Parables of Kierkegaard*, edited by Thomas C. Oden (Princeton, N.J.: Princeton University Press, 1978), pp. 51–52. Note that, as this parable illustrates, Kierkegaard does not use parable to grasp the inner nature of the God-man. Instead, he is concerned with our grasping the implications of the christological paradox *for our existence*. This sort of "grasping" of the issues, far from lessening the tension involved in the paradox, may actually serve to highlight the absurdity or extremity of the Christ-paradox.

It is worth thinking also about the various forms of paradox that may be involved in approaching Christ as the God-man. As we have seen, the basic paradox or category mistake is the assertion that the infinite God has become a finite human being in Jesus. This category mistake demands the imaginative stretching of our finite linguistic resources if we are to grasp it, however inadequately. We might wish to assert, for example, that Jesus as the Christ is the "Lamb of God." In other words, we might employ a symbolic expression. But this imaginative stretching may itself entail category mistakes. Paul Ricouer has suggested that metaphors, and by extension symbols, are built around something akin to a category mistake. (See Paul Ricouer, *Interpretation Theory: Discourse and the Surplus of Meaning* [Fort Worth, Tex.: Texas Christian University, 1976], p. 51.) When Shakespeare writes of "sleep that knits up the raveled sleeve of care," for example, he is creating category mistakes: sleep is not a knitter, and care is not a raveled sleeve. We might say, then, that while the assertion that Jesus is both God and man is a category mistake, it is nonetheless a literal formulation. But the metaphors or symbols employed to describe the God-man paradox, such as the statement that Christ is the Lamb of God, are category mistakes meant to fail on the literal level in such a way as to point us to a second level of meaning.

An alternative route would be to deny that Christ as the God-man confronts us with a real paradox or category mistake. In Karl Rahner's theological anthropology, for example, openness to God is a constitutive, albeit supernatural, element of human being. Thus the total openness to God that characterizes one who is both God and man does not represent a category mistake, the putting together of two things that do not belong together, but rather the perfect fulfillment of human being. The fact that Jesus is God confronts us with a mystery, then, but not with a contradiction. Thus, in the first volume of his *Theological Investigations*, Rahner asserts: "Only someone who forgets that the essence of man is to be unbounded . . . can suppose that it is impossible for there to be a man who, precisely by being man in the fullest sense (which we never attain) is God's existence into the world." Quoted in Macquarrie, *Jesus Christ in Modern Thought*, p. 370.

33. John Locke, "Essay Concerning Human Understanding," in *Eighteenth-Century Philosophy*, edited by Lewis White Beck (New York: Free Press, 1966), p. 57.

34. Hans Georg Gadamer, *Truth and Method*, translation edited by Garret Barden and John Cumming (New York: Continuum, 1975), p. 102.

35. John Macquarrie, *Jesus Christ in Modern Thought*, p. 16.

36. Ibid., p. 17. Note, however, that Gadamer's own concern is not with the production of the work of art as much as with how the one who encounters it is taken up into the work in a way that goes beyond his or her subjectivity. Hence his famous analogy of being taken up into the playing of a game.

37. Note that this issue of grasping and expressing the revelation is distinct from the preceding issue, that is, deciding via human reason that an alleged revelation is in fact a revelation. I do not in all instances have to grasp the content of a revelation in order to judge it to be a revelation. I might, for example, decide that the claim of a certain authority that event "a" is a revelation, is a good reason for me to accept the idea that event "a" is a revelation. In such a case, I must still employ my own reason to decide that I shall accept event "a" as a revelation, but this use of reason does not necessarily involve my grasping or being able to express the content of the revelation.

But now consider a different situation, one in which I decide that something is a revelation not on the basis of authority or tradition, but because I myself "recognize" the event as a revelation. What would it mean for me to claim, for example, that I recognize Jesus as God? Would it mean that I experience God in Jesus? But doesn't that suggest the possibility that there is a way around imaginative construction after all? To attempt to grasp the paradox of the God-man requires a leap of creative imagination, but I decide that Jesus is the God-man and attempt to grasp that reality because I have already recognized Jesus as God by experiencing God in him. Thus, this experience of God in Jesus seems to involve a more direct access to the divine, an access that precedes the act of imaginative construction and stimulates it. This would be to misunderstand the situation, however. There is no such thing as raw experience; all experience presupposes some kind of cognitive framework to make it possible, to form it as an experience of one particular kind rather than another. Experience of God is no different. Thus, to experience God in Jesus is to have already done the constructive work entailed in accepting a Christ of faith; it is to have responded in an attitude of faith to Jesus and to have accepted him as the Christ.

Yet ought there not exist some *reason* why I take Jesus to be the Christ and believe that God is incarnate in him? Even if I do not experience God in Jesus prior to the act of faith in Christ, something must lead me to that act of faith. It is clear, first of all, that I must already have some notion of God prior to deciding to accept Jesus as God, or the very idea of accepting him as God would be without meaning. I will decide, for one reason or another, that what I see in Jesus is consistent with this notion of God, or perhaps that there is an initial consistency, but that Jesus goes beyond my notion of God in such a way as to deepen it. But if this already existing notion of God (or some prior experience of God) that I bring to my encounter with Jesus entails anything more than negative knowledge about God—that God is unlimited, for example—or relational knowledge about God—that God is the cause of goodness, for instance—then that notion will itself have been the product of imaginative construction in the sense that has been discussed above.

Consider a concrete illustration of this whole process. Suppose that I see in the life of Jesus a radical love ethic, a way of life that throws away all calculation as to what one owes the neighbor. Christ would have us love our enemies and give the neighbor more than he or she asks. Let us say that this ethic of love without calculation of cost to oneself, which I see lived out in the person of Jesus, negates the whole way of being that characterizes ordinary human behavior. As a result, Jesus' way of being is tantamount to a transcendence of the "world" constituted by human calculations of self-interest. This is not yet, strictly speaking, to see God in Jesus. We are not confronted with God directly, but experience in Jesus the negation of our everyday ethical world. And this provides the warrant for a subsequent act of constructive discernment, an act in which one can accept Jesus as the Christ, that is, imaginatively construe Christ as God. In order to make the move from seeing the negation of the ordinary world in Jesus to imaginatively grasping him as God presupposes that I already have some concept of God as that which transcends mundane reality.

There is a related matter that must be considered here in order to understand what is involved in seeing Jesus as the Christ. The illustration we have just considered, in which one encounters in Jesus the transcendence of the ordinary world of human ethical calculation, is most straightforwardly applicable, not to contemporary Christians, but to those persons in the first century who actually met Jesus of Nazareth. The situation of later generations of Christians involves one or more additional layers. Later Christians construe Jesus as the Christ only after he has already been accepted as the Christ by others and presented to them by the tradition of the church as such. We might say that they accept Jesus Christ as the Christ. This may simply involve appropriating for oneself, in an attitude of faith, an already existing model of the Christ. In some other situations, it may involve a community, or perhaps even a particular individual, responding to earlier imaginative models of Christ by creating new Christs of faith. Thus, the history of Christianity includes whole chains of Christs of faith: Jesus' original followers responded to him by creating various Christs of faith; later Christians were confronted by Jesus in the form of these Christs of faith, to which they responded with their own models of Christ, and so on down through the centuries of the Christian tradition.

38. The world's religions frequently suggest that the attempt to know the infinite taxes our cognitive resources. To vary the familiar Taoist dictum slightly, the Tao that can be named is not the infinite Tao. But it is not entirely clear that the notion of the infinite has any meaning. Do we actually have a concept of the infinite, as Descartes maintained? Or, does the notion of the infinite amount to nothing more than an empty gesture based on the mistaken assumption that, because the notion of the finite makes sense, it must be meaningful to talk about something that is not finite? In using the word "infinite" to refer to the transcendent reality at issue in the Christian religion, it is useful, I think, to take a phenomenological tack. That is, the concept "infinite" refers to what is experienced as transforming the finite. A paradigmatic example within the Christian tradition might be the experience of redemption, wherein, so Christianity claims, the power of sin is in some sense conquered. While the tradition does not equate finitude with sin—the finite order was created good—the fallenness of the finite world results in the fact that only something beyond the finite can rescue it from the power of sin. This phenomenological avenue to the infinite, which makes use of dialectical interpretations of infinity—the infinite is the negation of the negativities of the finite—also allows us to make sense of the claim that the kind of radically nonmetaphysical versions of God that will be touched upon in chapter 3 put us in touch with something "infinite."

39. Josef Rupert Geiselmann, *The Meaning of Tradition*, translated by W. J. O'Hara, *Quaestiones Disputatae* 15 (Freiburg: Herder, 1966), p. 12.

40. The expression "blank wonder" is one of Rudolph Otto's descriptions of the experience of the divine. See his *The Idea of the Holy: An Inquiry into the Non-Rational Factor in the Idea of the Divine and Its Relation to the Rational*, translated by John W. Harvey (New York: Oxford, 1958), p. 26.

41. See Karl Barth, *The Epistle to the Romans*, translated by Edwyn C. Hoskyns (New York: Oxford, 1968). Tillich holds that "every type of faith has the tendency to elevate its concrete symbols to absolute validity. The criterion of the truth of faith, therefore, is that it implies an element of self-negation. That symbol is most adequate which expresses not only the ultimate but also its own lack of ultimacy. Christianity expresses itself in such a symbol . . . in the Cross of Christ. Jesus could not have been the Christ without sacrificing himself as Jesus to himself as the Christ." Paul Tillich, *Dynamics of Faith* (New York: Harper & Row, 1957), p. 97.

42. Imagination has an even larger role to play, no doubt, in those artistic depictions of Jesus that actually add words and events to the New Testament accounts in order to more fully realize Jesus as an individual. One thinks here of Nikos Kazantzakis' *The Last Temptation of Christ* (translated by P. A. Bien [New York: Simon & Schuster, 1960]), and of Martin Scorsese's film version of the novel. For a more recent example, see James Carse, *The Gospel of the Beloved Disciple* (San Francisco: Harper San Francisco, 1997).

43. Having detailed the various ways in which what I am calling imaginative construction enters into the creation of Christs of faith, it is now appropriate for me to clarify the relation of my position to Gordon Kaufman's well-known discussion of imagination and theological construction. It should be noted, first of all, that Kaufman is principally concerned with constructing the concept or symbol of God, while I am obviously focusing on Christ-construction. Not all of the ways that I have listed above in which imagination enters the project of Christ-construction are directly related to the matter of conceiving God. However, it is certainly true that the most insistent demand that our ordinary categories of thought be imaginatively stretched when we talk about the Christ derives from the fact that the Christ is believed to be a manifestation of the infinite, that is, of God. Thus, Kaufman's analysis of imaginative construction of the notion of God is by no means irrelevant to the present discussion.

There are some potentially surprising elements, as well as several significant ambiguities, in Kaufman's most thorough treatment of the imaginative construction of our notion of God, which he undertakes in his *In Face of Mystery: A Constructive Theology* (Cambridge: Harvard University Press, 1993). Kaufman wants our talk about God to be talk about our experience of the ordinary world, rather than about a supernatural reality. Hence, he connects the notion of God with the serendipitous creativity evident in the evolutionary process that has led to human life and that continues to support it. Yet, despite this focus on the mundane, Kaufman puts a great deal of emphasis on the mysteriousness of what we encounter and on our inability finally to grasp it: "our 'knowledge' of this world in which we live, and all the realities within it, always shades off into ultimate mystery, into an ultimate unknowing" (p. 326). Indeed, the mystery is sufficiently deep for Kaufman to hold that, when we make claims about the reality that he identifies with God, "we really do not know what we are saying" (p. xii).

Note two potentially problematic aspects of this approach to the divine mystery. First, it stands in significant contrast to the notion of God's mysteriousness found in more traditional theologies. It is clear that we possess a significant scientific knowledge of the evolutionary process that has produced the human species. But Kaufman suggests that when we attempt to plumb the existential significance of this process and what lies behind it, the components that deserve to be identified with divinity, we are nearly bereft of knowledge. By contrast, more traditional theologies usually ground their recognition of divine mystery in what amounts to an initial, significant body of knowledge about God. Thus, a traditional theologian might begin with the conviction that God is an omnipotent being who has created the universe. Given the awareness of divine majesty that follows from this knowledge, the theologian will go on to claim that when we speak of God's personhood, for example, we must recognize that divine personhood far transcends our own limited notions of what it means to be a person. As a result, we must employ our notion of person analogously when we apply it to God. That is, we recognize that divine personhood is mysterious precisely as a result of our knowing something about God, such as that he is the all-powerful creator of the universe. Kaufman, by contrast, often speaks as if we know almost nothing about God, that mystery is a function of nearly complete ignorance.

The second matter worthy of concern here, an issue closely related to the preceding one, is Kaufman's linkage of divine mystery and the use of symbols for God (he speaks constantly of "the symbol 'God'"). Certainly divine mystery and symbols go together. Symbols are nonliteral forms of communication. Because the divine transcends our cognitive grasp, the best we can do in attempting to refer to the divine is imaginatively to stretch the limited cognitive resources at our disposal. One important way in which to do this is to employ symbols when talking about God, since symbols work by pushing us beyond literal formulations of our relation to reality. But Kaufman's emphasis on radical mystery threatens to short-circuit the mechanism of symbolic meaning. Here is the issue: I must have a modicum of knowledge about God, knowledge that can be expressed in literal terms, in order subsequently to be able to recognize something as a symbol of God, and to know in what sense the symbol is operating symbolically rather than literally. (Cf. Wilbur Urban's chastisement of Tillich for initially claiming that *all* statements about God are symbolic, a chastisement that Tillich took seriously. See Wilbur Urban, "Prof. Tillich's Theory of the Religious Symbol," *Journal of Liberal Religion* 2 [Summer 1940]: 36; and Paul Tillich, "Reply to Interpretation and Criticism," in *The Theology of Paul Tillich*, 2d ed., edited by Charles W. Kegley [New York: Pilgrim Press, 1982], p. 379.) Kaufman sometimes appears to be both aware of and unconcerned about this potential difficulty: "we really do not know precisely what it is in the world-process to which these [theological] metaphors refer. Faith believes *that* they refer, but to what they refer remains in many respects mystery" (p. 331).

In any case, this radical emphasis on mystery in Kaufman's theology implies an equally radical and thoroughgoing version of imaginative construction. Our theological constructions will necessarily be less an imaginative *response to* what we know is "out there," and more a matter of *taking the initiative* with our imagination. Hence, the very unity of what we will regard as the divine reality may turn out to be not just approached through, but actually created by, our imagination: the symbol "God," says Kaufman, "sums up, unifies, and represents in a personification what are taken to be the highest and most indispensable human ideals and values" (p. 311). I have no problem with this kind of radical theological proposal; I only wish that Kaufman were clearer about whether this is indeed what he has in mind. He could do much to aid his readers' understanding, for example, by specifying the relation of his own position to that of John Dewey in *A Common Faith* (New Haven: Yale University Press, 1934).

The need for imagination in the construction of Christs is based, in part, on the need for imagination in constructing the notion of God. I have indicated here what I take to be a few potential ambiguities and problems in Kaufman's notion of imaginative theological construction. In addition, it should be noted that Kaufman's approach is, appropriately enough, just one particular interpretation of the role of imagination in thinking about God. Given my concern in this book with pluralism, I do not wish arbitrarily to limit the number of theories about theological imagination. There are many notions of God, just as there are many notions of the Christ, and, in a discussion of the ramifications of christological pluralism, we should not choose among those notions of God. The Thomist's use of imagination in employing analogous language about God, for example, is as relevant for our purposes as Kaufman's use of imagination in his theology.

CHAPTER TWO. TRADITION AND SUBTRADITIONS

1. Jacquelyn Grant, *White Women's Christ and Black Women's Jesus: Feminist Christology and Womanist Response*, American Academy of Religion Academy Series, no. 64 (Atlanta: Scholars Press, 1989), p. 3.

2. Gadamer, *Truth and Method*, p. 324.

3. Ibid., p. 239.

4. Ibid., p. 246.

5. Philemon vv. 10–17.

6. James Cone provides telling evidence from Augustine and Thomas Aquinas in this regard: "According to Augustine, slavery was due to the sinfulness of the slaves. Therefore he admonished 'slaves to be subject to their masters . . . ,' serving 'them with a good-heart and a good-will. . . .' For Thomas, slavery was a part of the natural order of creation. Thus 'the slave, in regard to his master, is an instrument. . . . Between a master and his slave there is a special right of domination.'" James Cone, *God of the Oppressed* (New York: Seabury, 1975), p. 198.

7. Pope John Paul II, *Encyclical Letter,* Veritatis Splendor, *Addressed by the Supreme Pontiff Pope John Paul II to All the Bishops of the Catholic Church Regarding Certain Fundamental Questions of the Church's Moral Teaching* (Washington, D.C.: United States Catholic Conference, 1993), p. 51.

8. Ibid., p. 52.

9. As with many other aspects of the search for genuine Christs, we must acknowledge the necessity of interpretation where the notion of subtraditions is concerned, rather than supposing that we can find any absolute criteria for determining just which groups constitute genuine subtraditions of the larger Christian tradition. For example, what are we to make of the differences between the Church of Jesus Christ of Latter Day Saints and other denominations? Is Mormon theology sufficiently unique that the Mormon church should be considered a separate religion rather than a subdivision of the larger Christian tradition, or does that theology constitute the kind of legitimate challenge from a subtradition to the larger church that is essential for the continuing development of the Christian tradition? And if we do acknowledge a particular group as a legitimate subtradition of the larger church, how exactly do we grasp the identifying boundaries of that group? This may pose no great problem where particular denominations are concerned, such as the Presbyterian Church or the

Roman Catholic Church, for example, since such denominations present us with *institutional* boundaries. But how are we to discern the boundaries of something such as "African-American Christianity," which might be taken as a particular subtradition of the larger whole?

10. Pelikan, *Jesus Through the Centuries*, p. 132.

11. The claim that a tradition maintains identity through difference is hardly unprecedented, of course, and has numerous secular instantiations, where there can be no appeal to providential guidance. In U.S. law, for example, the courts use the Constitution to test and limit legislation (akin to the larger tradition limiting the Christs of the subtraditions). But the most significant cases result not just in the dictates of the Constitution being applied mechanically to a new law, but entail new interpretations of the Constitution itself (analogous to how the subtraditions act back upon the larger tradition). This means that the Constitution that is brought to bear on legislation in the future will not be entirely the same as the Constitution of the past. But this interpretive movement is regarded not as a corruption of the Constitution but as its growth. In other words, we encounter here a claim of identity in difference as development.

12. See Friedrich Schleiermacher, *The Christian Faith*, translation edited by H. R. Mackintosh and J. S. Stewart (Philadelphia: Fortress, 1928; 1976), pp. 391–98.

13. *The Myth of God Incarnate*, edited by John Hick (Philadelphia: Westminster, 1977).

14. See Peter Berger, *The Sacred Canopy: Elements of a Sociological Theory of Religion* (Garden City, N.Y.: Doubleday-Anchor, 1967).

15. David Tracy, *The Analogical Imagination: Christian Theology and the Culture of Pluralism* (New York: Crossroad, 1981), p. 100.

16. For an account of the relevance of contemporary antifoundationalism to theology, see John E. Thiel, *Nonfoundationalism* (Minneapolis: Augsburg Fortress, 1994).

17. See, for instance, Alvin Plantinga, "Is Belief in God Properly Basic?" *Nous* 15 (March 1981): 41–51, and "Reason and Belief in God," in *Faith and Rationality: Reason and Belief in God*, edited by Alvin Plantinga and Nicholas Wolterstorff (Notre Dame: University of Notre Dame Press, 1983), pp. 16–93. George A. Lindbeck, *The Nature of Doctrine: Religion and Theology in a Postliberal Age* (Philadelphia: Westminster, 1984).

18. The foundationalist's criteria for proper basicality are internally or self-referentially incoherent in that the claim that one's basic beliefs must be evident to the senses, or self-evident, or incorrigible, is a claim that is not itself evident to the senses, or self-evident, or incorrigible.

19. Thus, there are *grounds* for my belief that I had breakfast this morning, but that belief is not a conclusion drawn from evidence. That is, my belief that I had breakfast this morning is not a belief that rests on other beliefs: it is a basic belief.

20. To be more precise, a belief such as the one that God exists may not itself be properly basic for the Christian, but it is entailed by a belief that is properly basic, such as the belief that God loves me.

21. Lindbeck, *The Nature of Doctrine*, p. 49.

22. I have attempted to indicate some potential difficulties with Plantinga's position in my "Theism and Proper Basicality: A Response to Plantinga," *International Journal for Philosophy of Religion* 14 (1983): 123–27, and "The Crucial Disanalogies between Properly Basic Belief and Belief in God," *Religious Studies* 26 (1990): 389–401. For important critiques of Lindbeck's position, see David Tracy, "Lindbeck's New Program for Theology: A Reflection," *The Thomist* 49 (1985): 460–72, and Timothy P. Jackson, "Against Grammar," *Religious Studies Review* 11 (1985): 240–45.

23. Lindbeck does allow for the possibility that "religions may be complementary in the sense that they provide guidance to different but not incompatible dimensions of existence. Perhaps, for example, Buddhists know more about contemplation, and Christians about social action, and perhaps they can learn from each other in these domains even while retaining their categorially different notions of the maximally important." See *The Nature of Doctrine*, p. 53. But note that such complementarity has to do with Buddhism and Christianity contributing to "*different*" dimensions of one's existence. By contrast, my example suggests the possibility of Buddhism contributing to the Christian's understanding of the very dimension of existence addressed by the Christian notion of sin.

24. Plantinga argues, via a discussion of how "fideism" should be defined, that his own position is not, in fact, a species of fideism. See "Reason and Belief in God," pp. 87–90.

25. Lest I be accused of an old-fashioned kind of interdenominational polemic here, I must point out that my own tradition is Protestant.

26. See "Dogmatic Constitution *Dei Filius* on the Catholic Faith," in *Documents of Vatican Council I*, selected and translated by John F. Broderick, S.J. (Collegeville, Minn.: Liturgical Press, 1971), pp. 37–52. Note the assertion, for example, that "God, the beginning and end of all things, can be known with certitude by the natural light of human reason from created things" (p. 41).

27. See, for example, the following of his recent works: *After Virtue: A Study in Moral Philosophy* (Notre Dame: University of Notre Dame, 1981); *Whose Justice? Which Rationality?* (Notre Dame: University of Notre Dame, 1988); *Three Rival Versions of Moral Philosophy* (Notre Dame: University of Notre Dame, 1990).

28. MacIntyre, *Whose Justice?*, p. 12.

29. Though Max Stackhouse is correct, I think, in holding that "such a possibility [of traditions evaluating one another] invites new levels of reflection about some generic epistemic capacity that MacIntyre does not seem to have fully faced." See his "Alasdair MacIntyre: An Overview and Evaluation," *Religious Studies Review* 18 (1992): 204.

30. Catholic theologians usually distinguish, of course, between Tradition—the part of Catholic belief and practice revealed by God—and tradition—the purely human customs and assumptions that are necessarily also a part of the church's life.

31. Yves M.-J. Congar, *Tradition and Traditions: An Historical Essay and a Theological Essay*, translated by Michael Naseby and Thomas Rainborough (New York: Macmillan, 1967), p. 8.

32. The universal intent of Catholic tradition, and of the Christian tradi-

tion generally, gives added support to David Tracy's contention that theology is and ought to be a "public" undertaking, with several different publics involved. See especially *The Analogical Imagination*.

33. "Pastoral Constitution on the Church in the Modern World," in *The Documents of Vatican II*, edited by Walter M. Abbott, S.J. and Joseph Gallagher (Washington, D.C.: America Press, 1966), p. 209.

34. John Paul II, *Fides et Ratio*, *Origins* 28 (October 22, 1998): 317–48.

CHAPTER THREE. CHRIST-TESTING

1. See, for example, Anne E. Carr, *Transforming Grace: Christian Tradition and Women's Experience* (San Francisco: Harper & Row, 1988), p. 186.

2. It is important to qualify this preference for the canonical gospels, however, especially given our focus on pluralism. It is surely true that the noncanonical gospels are less effective than the canonical in keeping us in touch with what the bulk of Christians through the ages have meant by Christ. But they are undoubtedly *more* effective than the canonical gospels in putting us in communication with minority voices, which ought also to be heard in any attempt to construe the Christ.

3. See Paul Tillich, *Systematic Theology* 2:102–38.

4. The expression "oldest Roman catechism" is applied to the Apostle's Creed in the *Catechism of the Catholic Church*, p. 53 (paragraph 196). The text of the Creed is reproduced on pp. 49–50 of the *Catechism*.

5. Ibid., p. 49.

6. Bernard Lonergan, *The Way to Nicea: the Dialectical Development of Trinitarian Theology*, translated by Conn O'Donovan (Philadelphia: Westminster, 1976), p. 103.

7. We shall bracket the fact here that salvation can be conceived in innumerable ways. The Christian approach to salvation is circular, of course, in that the claim that Christ provides salvation is dependent on a view of what constitutes salvation that is itself a function of faith in Christ.

8. For a trenchant treatment of the relation of christologies and power, see Elisabeth Schüssler Fiorenza, *Jesus: Miriam's Child, Sophia's Prophet—Critical Issues in Feminist Christology* (New York: Continuum, 1995).

9. A. N. Williams reminds us that "deification became the dominant model of salvation and sanctification in the patristic period." See her "Deification in the *Summa Theologiae*: A Structural Interpretation of the *Prima Pars*," in *The Thomist* 61(1997): 220. The burden of the article cited here is her argument that deification is still alive and well in Aquinas' theology. For further evidence that *theosis* survives in later Western theology, see Dennis Bielfeldt, "Deification as a Motif in Luther's *Dictata super psalterium*," in *The Sixteenth Century Journal* 28 (Summer 1997): 401–20.

10. See Rahner, *Foundations of Christian Faith*, chapter 6. Rahner does make some technical distinctions about just how openness to God is a part of our being. Following Heidegger, he refers to the definitive characteristics of human being, in distinction from the attributes of other kinds of being, as "exis-

tentials." Insofar as the unthematic awareness of God is a presupposition of all of our knowing and doing, it is properly considered an existential. Yet it is not like the other existentials that constitute our nature. Rather, as the constant, gracious act of God in relation to us, his continually making himself present, it is a "supernatural existential." See ibid., pp. 126–33.

11. Schleiermacher, *The Christian Faith*, p. 385.

12. Jürgen Moltmann, *The Way of Jesus Christ: Christology in Messianic Dimensions*, translated by Margaret Kohl (San Francisco: HarperCollins, 1990), p. xiii.

13. See Mircea Eliade, *The Sacred and the Profane: The Nature of Religion*, translated by Willard R. Trask (New York: Harcourt, Brace and World, 1959).

14. See *The Myth of God Incarnate*, edited by John Hick.

15. Frances Young, "A Cloud of Witnesses," in ibid., p. 31.

16. Ibid., p. 37.

17. Dennis Nineham, "Epilogue," in ibid., p. 201.

18. See, for example, Friedrich Schleiermacher, *The Christian Faith*; Karl Rahner, *Foundations of Christian Faith*; Paul Tillich, *Systematic Theology*, vol. 1; John B. Cobb and David Ray Griffin, *Process Theology: An Introductory Exposition* (Philadelphia: Westminster, 1976).

19. See, for instance, Gordon D. Kaufmann, *The Theological Imagination*, and *In Face of Mystery*; Sallie McFague, *Metaphorical Theology: Models of God in Religious Language* (Philadelphia: Fortress, 1982), and *Models of God: Theology for an Ecological, Nuclear Age* (Philadelphia: Fortress, 1987).

20. See Ludwig Feuerbach, *The Essence of Christianity*, translated by George Eliot (New York: Harper & Row, 1957); Sigmund Freud, *The Future of an Illusion*, edited and translated by James Strachey (New York: Norton, 1961).

21. See John Dewey, *A Common Faith* (New Haven: Yale University Press, 1934).

22. See my "Enacting the Divine: Feminist Theology and the Being of God," *The Journal of Religion* 74 (October 1994): 506–23, and *When God Becomes Goddess: The Transformation of American Religion* (New York: Continuum, 1995).

23. Schillebeeckx, *Jesus*, p. 586.

24. Ibid., p. 604.

25. Even for thinkers who embrace the model of God as a supernatural consciousness who periodically intervenes in the world, the expression, "God *decides* to reveal himself in Jesus," may need to be taken as analogical or symbolic, in that God's eternity and omniscience preclude God from making a decision in the way that human beings consider their options and subsequently decide to act.

26. A religious perspective according to which human beings enact the divine, such as the one I have attributed above to thinkers such as Rosemary Ruether and Carol Christ, obviously sees the divine as a function of human being, however much it may also hold that God can transcend us. And for theologians such as Kaufman and McFague, it is clear that our *access* to God, at least, is largely dependent upon our own powers. But even Tillich's version of

panentheism defines the being of God in terms of God's relation to human being: God is there conceived, in good transcendental phenomenological fashion, as the "depth" of the self-world structure of being, the structure that is the condition of the possibility for all human experience. See my *Symbol and Empowerment: Paul Tillich's Post-Theistic System* (Macon, Ga.: Mercer University Press, 1985).

27. Note, however, that it would be possible, if unlikely, for one to opt for a nonprovidential view of Christ while holding that God is a personal consciousness. Such a Christ would reveal God even though God had made no special initiative to reveal himself in the Christ and despite the fact that this God *could* have made such an initiative if God had seen fit to do so.

28. It is also possible to imagine combining a providentialist view of Christ with the notion that what is revealed in the Christ is not limited to Jesus. In this perspective, God chooses to reveal Godself in the Buddha, Krishna, the Christ, and others, but does not intend any one of these revelations to be definitive in an exclusivist sense. The point at issue now, however, is that if one adopts a *non*-providentialist view of the Christ, it will seem *particularly* plausible that what is revealed in the Christ need not be limited to Jesus as the Christ.

29. It is important to recognize too, however, that our human categories of thought and expression cannot be *thoroughly* inadequate. If there were nothing about those categories that allowed them to point us toward the transcendent, then of course we could know nothing at all about God through them, however willing we were to recognize their inadequacy.

30. See Rosemary Radford Ruether, *Sexism and God-Talk: Toward a Feminist Theology* (Boston: Beacon, 1983).

31. Rosemary Radford Ruether, "Can Christology Be Liberated from Patriarchy?" in *Reconstructing the Christ Symbol: Essays in Feminist Christology*, edited by Maryanne Stevens (New York: Paulist, 1993), p. 24.

32. Ruether, *Sexism and God-Talk*, p. 131.

33. Ibid., 138.

34. Ibid.

35. Rita Nakashima Brock, "Losing Your Innocence But Not Your Hope," in Stevens, ed., *Reconstructing the Christ Symbol*, p. 48.

36. See *The New Hermeneutics*, edited by James M. Robinson and John B. Cobb Jr. (New York: Harper & Row, 1964).

37. Italo Calvino, *If on a winter's night a traveler*, translated by William Weaver (New York: Harcourt Brace Jovanovich, 1981), p. 155.

38. See, for example, Emmanuel Levinas, *Otherwise than Being or Beyond Essence*, translated by Alphonso Lingis (The Hague: Martinus Nijhoff, 1981).

39. Thomas Jefferson, letter to James Smith, December 8, 1822, in *The Life and Selected Writings of Thomas Jefferson*, edited by Adrienne Koch and William Peden (New York: Modern Library, 1993), p. 642.

40. Quoted in E. Forrester Church, "The Gospel According to Thomas Jefferson," in Thomas Jefferson, *The Jefferson Bible: The Life and Morals of Jesus of Nazareth* (Boston: Beacon, 1989), p. 30.

41. See ibid.

42. The date of completion is E. Forrester Church's calculation in "The Gospel According to Thomas Jefferson," pp. 26–28.

43. Ralph Waldo Emerson, "An Address," in *The Selected Writings of Ralph Waldo Emerson*, edited by Brooks Atkinson (New York: Modern Library, 1992), p. 64.

44. Ibid., p. 68.

45. Ibid., p. 69.

46. Paul M. van Buren, *The Secular Meaning of the Gospel: Based on an Analysis of Its Language* (New York: Macmillan, 1963; paperback edition), p. 103.

47. Ibid., p. 141.

48. George W. Forell, *The Proclamation of the Gospel in a Pluralistic World* (Philadelphia: Fortress, 1973), p. 44.

49. See Peter L. Berger, "For a World with Windows," in *Against the World for the World: The Hartford Appeal and the Future of American Religion*, edited by Peter L. Berger and Richard John Neuhaus (New York: Seabury, 1976), pp. 8–19.

50. Both the emphasis on biological destiny and the emphasis on the effect of environment on our personal development have contributed to the "culture of victimhood" much decried by some critics of contemporary American culture. The reference below to contextualized responsibility is intended to take seriously the decentering effects of biology and environment without falling prey to the excesses of the culture of victimhood.

51. Why call this reading "secondary"? If centerdness must include freedom in the fullest sense, then the fallen self can never be centered. For the fallen self is beset by sin in such a way that it is not free to achieve the purpose that God intends for it. Thus the fallen, sinful self can be understood as centered only by employing a secondary or weaker sense of centeredness: the power of sin unifies the self, for example, by providing the desire to be one's own master, in isolation from God, as a consistent source of one's actions.

52. Though one could also read the self here as centered, but thoroughly in bondage to sin.

53. See Martin Heidegger, *Being and Time*, translated by John Macquarrie and Edward Robinson (New York: Harper & Row, 1962).

54. His classic statement is *Moral Man and Immoral Society: A Study in Ethics and Politics* (New York: Scribner's, 1932).

55. Hermann Cohen, *Religion of Reason out of the Sources of Judaism*, translated by Simon Kaplan (New York: Frederick Ungar, 1972), p. 82. The original German edition appeared posthumously in 1919.

56. See Paul Tillich, *Systematic Theology* 1:59–66.

57. David Tracy, *Blessed Rage for Order: The New Pluralism in Theology* (New York: Seabury, 1975)

58. Norman Vincent Peale, *The Power of Positive Thinking*, p. x.

59. Ibid., p. 16.

60. Ibid., p. 41.

61. Ibid., p. xi.

62. Ibid., p. 47.

63. Quoted in Martin E. Marty, *Modern American Religion*, vol. 3: *Under God, Indivisible—1941–1960* (Chicago: University of Chicago, 1996), p. 346.

CHAPTER FOUR. BLACK CHRISTS

1. Derrick Bell, *Faces at the Bottom of the Well: The Permanence of Racism* (New York: Basic Books, 1992), p. 190. Equally depressing, parallel figures can easily be added to those adduced by Bell. For instance, while African-Americans constitute only one-eighth of the U.S. population, they take up about one-half of the places in U.S. prisons. Young black men are also on the receiving end of crime in disproportionate numbers: a University of Pennsylvania medical school study showed that, over a four-year span, 40 percent of the young black men who lived in Philadelphia's inner city ended up in hospital emergency rooms as the result of a violent assault. The figures are quoted in Nicholas Lemann's review essay, "Justice for Blacks?" in *The New York Review of Books*, March 5, 1998, p. 25. Health is another arena in which one encounters troubling figures. At the end of the 1990s, according to the *New York Times*, various studies reported that "African-Americans contract most major diseases sooner than whites and die six or seven years sooner. Government statistics show long-stubborn black-white gaps are getting even bigger for diabetes, maternal mortality, asthma and several forms of cancer." And a study of similarly insured white and black Americans with coronary artery disease, published in 1997, "found that the blacks received significantly less aggressive care. Blacks . . . were 34 percent less likely to receive the most sophisticated diagnostic procedures and 67 percent less likely to undergo bypass surgery." See Peter T. Kilborn, "Nashville Clinic Offers Case Study of Chronic Gap in Black and White Health," *New York Times*, March 21, 1998, p. A6.

2. James H. Cone, *Black Theology and Black Power* (New York: Seabury, 1969), p. 31.

3. Ibid., p. 140.

4. James H. Cone, *A Black Theology of Liberation*, Twentieth Anniversary Edition (Maryknoll, N.Y.: Orbis, 1990; original edition, 1970), p. 113.

5. Ibid. Latin American liberation theology is in agreement with Cone's interest in the historical Jesus as the means to avoid mere subjective projection in the production of Christs of faith. See, for instance, Jon Sobrino, S.J., *Christology at the Crossroads: A Latin American Approach*, translated by John Drury (Maryknoll, N.Y.: Orbis, 1978), pp. 351–3.

6. See, for example, James H. Cone, *God of the Oppressed*, p. 113.

7. Ibid., p. 143.

8. Cone, *Black Theology and Black Power*, p. 39.

9. Cone, *God of the Oppressed*, p. 152.

10. Ibid., p. 158.

11. Ibid., p. 160.

12. Cone, *Black Theology and Black Power*, p. 62.

13. Cone, *God of the Oppressed*, p. 151.

14. Quoted in Jacquelyn Grant, *White Women's Christ and Black Women's Jesus*, p. 204.

15. Ibid., p. 2. See also Jacquelyn Grant, "Womanist Theology: Black Women's Experience as a Source for Doing Theology, with Special Reference to Christology," in *Black Theology: A Documentary History*, vol. 2: *1980–1992*, edited by James H. Cone and Gayraud S. Wilmore (Maryknoll, N.Y.: Orbis, 1993), pp. 273–89.

16. Ibid., p. 197.

17. Ibid., p. 198.

18. Cone, in his later reflections, has acknowledged the need to widen black theology by addressing forces such as sexism and classism. In his preface to the 1986 edition of *A Black Theology of Liberation*, he says, "The most glaring limitation of *A Black Theology of Liberation* was my failure to be receptive to the problem of sexism in the black community and society as a whole" (Twentieth Anniversary Edition, p. xv). Cf. James H. Cone, *My Soul Looks Back* (Nashville, Tenn.: Abingdon, 1982), p. 115: "Racism, classism, sexism, and imperialism are interconnected, and none can be correctly understood and eventually defeated without simultaneous attention to the others."

19. Grant, *White Women's Christ and Black Women's Jesus*, p. 216.

20. See ibid., p. 220.

21. The reasoning that leads to this conclusion involves a confrontation with and rejection of a racist interpretation of the data. A disproportionate number of young black males gets in trouble with the law in the United States. What singles them out for this trouble? Is the phenomenon to be explained, either wholly or in part, as a function of personality traits that are inherent in the black male? Any such interpretation is, even in the most literal and dispassionate sense of the term, a "racist" explanation. What, then, are the alternative explanations? The most obvious is to say that black males are, as a group, disproportionately placed in circumstances in our society that make criminal behavior more likely.

22. Our discussion above of providential and nonprovidential Christs adds yet another wrinkle. While Cone and Grant seem clearly to be thinking in terms of providential Christs, could one not also put forth coherent versions of the black, liberating Christ that would understand that Christ in nonprovidentialist terms? How would the redemption proffered by the latter sort of black Christ differ from the redemption offered by providentialist black Christs?

23. Gayraud Wilmore, "A Revolution Unfulfilled, But Not Invalidated," in Cone, *A Black Theology of Liberation*, p. 155.

24. I shall speak below of "white Christs," and this expression needs some explanation, insofar as most Christians will probably object that their Christ is beyond identification with a particular race. First of all, despite the fact that one may well understand the transcendent Christ as beyond race, and in addition may acknowledge that the historical Jesus of Nazareth was not a white American, one nonetheless quite naturally imagines the Christ as like oneself. Cone and Grant do this openly by averring that Christ is black. Hence, white Americans too, when it comes not to their abstract concepts but to their concrete images of the Christ, will tend to construct the Christ in their own image. Furthermore, however they concretely symbolize the Christ for themselves, their

Christs will inevitably be "white" just in the sense that they are constructed out of white experience and sensibilities; their Christs manifest a white American perspective upon the world.

25. The English "crisis" derives, via Latin, from the Greek *krisis*, "turning point, from *krinein*, to separate, decide." (*The American Heritage Dictionary of the English Language*, edited by William Morris [New York: American Heritage, 1971], p. 314.) Note the connection of separating and deciding with judgment: one separates what is good from what is evil; one discerns or decides what is right.

26. Cardinal Joseph Ratziner, "Instruction on Certain Aspects of the 'Theology of Liberation,'" in Juan Luis Segundo, *Theology and the Church: A Response to Cardinal Ratzinger and a Warning to the Whole Church*, rev. ed., translated by John W. Diercksmeier (San Francisco: Harper & Row, 1970; paperback edition, 1987), p. 173.

27. See above, p. 110n.41.

28. This notion of the still-wounded Christ bears some resemblance to Lloyd Steffen's concept of "Christ unascended." Unfortunately, that concept has been worked out, thus far, only in a privately circulated paper. For Steffen's published christological reflections, see especially chapter 9 of *Executing Justice: The Moral Meaning of the Death Penalty* (Cleveland, Ohio: Pilgrim, 1998).

29. If one cannot in fact embrace a black Christ in this situation, so that one in effect simply defers to others who can, the power even of black Christs to redeem is undercut. If the crisis is a crisis for the whole society and not just for underclass African Americans, for example, then the whole society requires redemption. But if I cannot embrace the kind of Christ who redeems, then I and others like me are apparently cut off from that redemption.

30. To be more precise, one might say that this is an example of a subtradition acting back upon the larger tradition by affecting one or more other subtraditions, in that we have focused on the impact of black Christs upon white American Christianity, which is itself only one subtradition of the larger whole.

31. A contemporary philosophical analysis of what is involved in an immediate following of the Christ is provided by Robert P. Scharlemann in *The Reason of Following: Christology and the Ecstatic I* (Chicago: University of Chicago Press, 1995). Cf. note 32 below.

32. This kind of complementarity is a matter of seeing how it is possible to hold together the specific characteristics of different Christs. Another strategy for bringing order out of a potentially chaotic christological pluralism is to look for some one thing that a whole host of Christs has in common. One seeks to accomplish this by abstracting from the particularities of individual Christs. Thus, for example, Robert Scharlemann has argued that one can discern what he takes to be a christological form of reason, a "reason of following" exemplified in how each of Jesus' disciples encounters the disciple's own "I" outside himself in Jesus' call to follow him. While labeled "christological" because of its paradigmatic instantiation in Jesus' call to discipleship, this form of reason can be abstracted not just from different interpretations of the Christ, but from the figure of Jesus Christ altogether. While it is not in fact Scharlemann's stated goal

here to bring order out of a jumble of different Christs, this kind of move to a more abstract level of analysis might be adopted to that end. Similarly, John Cobb relates the figure of the Christ to contemporary Western pluralism by seeing the Christ as the principle of creative transformation within that society. In other words, instead of simply being subject to the forces that power pluralism, this Christ is himself the source of the transformative process that is contemporary pluralism. Although Cobb is not concerned with christological pluralism in particular, but rather with a more general pluralistic dynamic in our world, his project too can be understood as entailing a move to a higher level of abstraction, so that it is possible to see a christological dimension that transcends the differences of individual Christs. Indeed, in this scenario, Christ as the Logos can be read as the guiding principle behind the imaginative flowering of particular imaginary Christs. Our interpretive task is a different one, however. We seek to determine which Christs can be held in conversation with one another on the level of their specific and different attributes. See Robert P. Scharlemann, *The Reason of Following*, and John B. Cobb, *Christ in a Pluralistic Age* (Philadelphia: Westminster, 1975).

33. Note that "Christ is the Good Shepherd," for example, probably does not by itself constitute an imaginary Christ, but is a symbol that can be simply one part of one or more imaginary Christs.

CHAPTER FIVE. MY CHRIST, OTHER CHRISTS, AND THE BUDDHA

1. The notion of "the Christian community of which I am a part" might refer to a local congregation, a denominational body, or even the universal Christian community.

2. See, for example, Johann Adam Möhler's assertion that "Die Kirche ist gleichsam . . . die Entwicklung Christi in der Zeit" ["The Church is, as it were, . . . the development of Christ in time"]. *Wegbereiter heutiger Theologie*, edited by Heinrich Fries and Johann Finsterholzl, vol. 3: Johann Adam Möhler, edited by Paul-Werner Scheele (Vienna: Verlag Styria, 1969), p. 135.

3. This option may not be open to one who embraces a radically nonmetaphysical notion of the divine, such as might be attached to nonprovidential interpretations of the Christ. For if one does take a radically nonmetaphysical approach to God, as when one interprets God as a relation enacted by human beings, what prevents one from imagining and simultaneously embracing different models *of God*, just as we are here thinking about embracing different imaginary Christs? In that event, one's notion of God may not present the requisite unity.

4. As one significant example of the attempt seriously to wrestle with the relation of the Christ and the Buddha (from a Christian point of view) see Aloysius Pieris, S.J., *Love Meets Wisdom: A Christian Experience of Buddhism* (Maryknoll, N.Y.: Orbis, 1988).

5. Roy C. Amore, *Two Masters, One Message* (Nashville, Tenn.: Abingdon, 1978), p. 58.

6. John Cobb, "Can a Christian Be a Buddhist, Too?" *Japanese Religions* 10 (December 1978): 3.

7. Ibid., p. 18.

8. Ibid., p. 20.

9. Thich Nhat Hanh, *Living Buddha, Living Christ* (New York: Riverhead Books, 1995), p. 100.

SELECT BIBLIOGRAPHY

Amore, Roy C. *Two Masters, One Message.* Nashville, Tenn.: Abingdon, 1978.

Barth, Karl. *The Epistle to the Romans.* Translated by Edwyn C. Hoskyns. New York: Oxford, 1968.

Barton, Bruce. *The Man Nobody Knows: A Discovery of the Real Jesus.* Indianapolis: Bobbs-Merrill, 1925.

Bell, Derrick. *Faces at the Bottom of the Well: The Permanence of Racism.* New York: Basic Books, 1992.

Bellah, Robert. "Civil Religion in America." *Daedalus* 96 (Winter 1967): 1–21.

Bielfeldt, Dennis. "Deification as a Motif in Luther's *Dictata super psalterium.*" *The Sixteenth Century Journal* 28 (Summer 1997): 401–20.

Borg, Marcus J. *Jesus: A New Vision.* San Francisco: Harper & Row, 1987.

———. *Jesus in Contemporary Scholarship.* Valley Forge, Pa.: Trinity Press International, 1994.

Brown, Raymond E. *The Death of the Messiah: From Gethsemene to the Grave: A Commentary on the Passion Narratives in the Four Gospels.* New York: Doubleday, 1994.

Carr, Anne E. *Transforming Grace: Christian Tradition and Women's Experience.* San Francisco: Harper & Row, 1988.

Carse, James. *The Gospel of the Beloved Disciple.* San Francisco: Harper San Francisco, 1997.

Cobb, John B. *Christ in a Pluralistic Age.* Philadelphia: Westminster, 1975.

Cone, James H. *Black Theology and Black Power.* New York: Seabury, 1969.

———. *A Black Theology of Liberation.* Twentieth Anniversary Edition. Maryknoll, N.Y.: Orbis, 1990.

———. *God of the Oppressed.* New York: Seabury, 1975.

———. *My Soul Looks Back.* Nashville, Tenn.: Abingdon, 1982.

Congar, Yves M.-J. *Tradition and Traditions: An Historical Essay and a Theological Essay.* Translated by Michael Naseby and Thomas Rainborough. New York: Macmillan, 1967.

Crossan, John Dominic. *The Historical Jesus: The Life of a Mediterranean Jewish Peasant.* San Francisco: HarperCollins, 1991.

Gadamer, Hans-Georg. *Truth and Method.* Translation edited by Garret Barden and John Cumming. New York: Continuum, 1975.

Geiselmann, Josef Rupert. *The Meaning of Tradition.* Translated by W. J. O'Hara. *Quaestiones Disputatae* 15. Freiburg: Herder, 1966.

Grant, Jacquelyn. *White Women's Christ and Black Women's Jesus: Feminist Christology and Womanist Response.* American Academy of Religion Academy Series, no. 64. Atlanta: Scholars Press, 1989.

125

———. "Womanist Theology: Black Women's Experience as a Source for Doing Theology, with Special Reference to Christology." In *Black Theology: A Documentary History*, vol. 2: *1980–1992*, pp. 273–89. Edited by James H. Cone and Gayraud S. Wilmore. Maryknoll, N.Y.: Orbis, 1993.

Grigg, Richard. "Enacting the Divine: Feminist Theology and the Being of God." *The Journal of Religion* 74 (October 1994): 506–23.

———. *Symbol and Empowerment: Paul Tillich's Post-Theistic System*. Macon, Ga.: Mercer University Press, 1985.

———. *When God Becomes Goddess: The Transformation of American Religion*. New York: Continuum, 1995.

Hanh, Thich Nhat. *Living Buddha, Living Christ*. New York: Riverhead Books, 1995.

Hick, John, ed. *The Myth of God Incarnate*. Philadelphia: Westminister, 1997.

Jefferson, Thomas. *The Jefferson Bible: The Life and Morals of Jesus of Nazareth*. Boston: Beacon, 1989.

John Paul II. *Fides et Ratio*. Origins 28 (October 22, 1998): 317–48.

———. *Veritatis Splendor*. Washington D.C.: United States Catholic Conference, 1993.

Kähler, Martin. *The So-Called Historical Jesus and the Historic Biblical Christ*. Translated, edited, and with an introduction by Carl E. Braaten. Philadelphia: Fortress, 1964.

Kaufman, Gordon. *In Face of Mystery: A Constructive Theology*. Cambridge: Harvard University Press, 1993.

———. *The Theological Imagination: Constructing the Concept of God*. Philadelphia: Westminster, 1981.

Kazantzakis, Nikos. *The Last Temptation of Christ*. Translated by P. A. Bien. New York: Simon & Schuster, 1960.

Lonergan, Bernard. *The Way to Nicea: The Dialectical Development of Trinitarian Theology*. Translated by Conn O'Donovan. Philadelphia: Westminster, 1976.

Mackey, James P., ed. *Religious Imagination*. Edinburgh: Edinburgh University Press, 1986.

Macquarrie, John. *Jesus Christ in Modern Thought*. Philadelphia: Trinity Press International, 1990.

Mitchell, Stephen. *The Gospel According to Jesus: A New Translation and Guide to His Essential Teachings for Believers and Unbelievers*. New York: HarperCollins, 1991.

Moltmann, Jürgen. *The Way of Jesus Christ: Christology in Messianic Dimensions*. Translated by Margaret Kohl. San Francisco: HarperCollins, 1990.

Niebuhr, H. Richard. *Christ and Culture*. New York: Harper and Row, 1951.

Otto, Rudolph. *The Idea of the Holy: An Inquiry into the Non-Rational Factor in the Idea of the Divine and Its Relation to the Rational*. Translated by John W. Harvey. New York: Oxford, 1958.

Pelikan, Jaroslav. *Jesus Through the Centuries: His Place in the History of Culture*. New Haven: Yale University Press, 1985.

Pieris, Aloysius. *Love Meets Wisdom: A Christian Experience of Buddhism*. Maryknoll, N.Y.: Orbis, 1988.

Rahner, Karl. *Foundations of Christian Faith: An Introduction to the Idea of Christianity.* Translated by William V. Dych. New York: Seabury, 1978.

Raposa, Michael L. *Boredom and the Religious Imagination.* Charlottesville: University Press of Virginia, 1999.

Ricouer, Paul. *Interpretation Theory: Discourse and the Surplus of Meaning.* Fort Worth, Tex.: Texas Christian University, 1976.

Riley, Gregory J. *One Jesus, Many Christs: How Jesus Inspired Not One True Christianity, But Many; The Truth about Christian Origins.* San Francisco: HarperCollins, 1997.

Ruether, Rosemary Radford. *Sexism and God-Talk: Toward a Feminist Theology.* Boston: Beacon: 1983.

Scharlemann, Robert P. *The Reason of Following: Christology and the Ecstatic I.* Chicago: University of Chicago Press, 1995.

Schillebeeckx, Edward. *Jesus: An Experiment in Christology.* Translated by Huburt Hoskins. New York: Crossroad, 1979.

Schleiermacher, Friedrich. *The Christian Faith.* Translation edited by H. R. Mackintosh and J. S. Stewart. Philadelphia: Fortress, 1928; 1976.

Schüssler Fiorenza, Elisabeth. *Jesus: Miriam's Child, Sophia's Prophet—Critical Issues in Feminist Christology.* New York: Continuum, 1995.

Sobrino, Jon. *Christology at the Crossroads: A Latin American Approach.* Translated by John Drury. Maryknoll, N.Y.: Orbis, 1978.

Steffen, Lloyd. *Executing Justice: The Moral Meaning of the Death Penalty.* Cleveland, Ohio: Pilgrim, 1998.

Stevens, Maryanne, ed. *Reconstructing the Christ Symbol: Essays in Feminist Christology.* New York: Paulist, 1993.

Tatum, W. Barnes. *In Quest of Jesus: A Guidebook.* Atlanta: John Knox Press, 1982.

Thiel, John E. *Nonfoundationalism.* Minneapolis: Augsburg Fortress, 1994.

Tillich, Paul. *Dynamics of Faith.* New York: Harper & Row, 1957.

———. *Systematic Theology.* 3 vols. Chicago: University of Chicago Press, 1951–63.

Tracy, David. *The Analogical Imagination: Christian Theology and the Culture of Pluralism.* New York: Crossroad, 1981.

———. *Blessed Rage for Order: The New Pluralism in Theology.* New York: Seabury, 1975.

van Buren, Paul M. *The Secular Meaning of the Gospel: Based on an Analysis of Its Language.* New York: Macmillan, 1963.

Williams, A. N. "Deification in the *Summa Theologiae*: A Structural Interpretation of the *Prima Pars*." *The Thomist* 61 (1997): 219–55.

INDEX